The Impact of Di

By

SUSHIL CHAUHAN

ABSTRACT

As the dominance of Internet is tremendously increasing with a pace. Customers are getting engaged with internet more and making use of digital devices to spend maximum of their times. They are making use of different social media channels for the communication purpose, they are using different platforms for study purpose, booking their traveling online and last but not the least using digital platforms for shopping purposes. All in all, the maximum of the daily activities is turning out to be online.

As the world is going digital, business organisations have also started looking for online platforms to expand their businesses. They are seeing a great scope in digitalisation. Business organisations have started using digital technologies for the advertisement and promotional activities. They are using different modes of digital marketing for this purpose. Digital marketing is acting as a catalyst and an enabler to boost the marketing and promotional activities within the organisation.

As India has started following the different schemes of Government like "Start-up India", "Make in India", "Stand-up India" and "Digital India", individuals are thinking of starting their own ventures, start-ups. In this, Digital Marketing can be a very much effective, efficient and helpful aspect for the growth of their start-up or business. These things generate a curiosity to study the different impacts of digital marketing with their motivational factors as well as the challenges in the adoption so that it can be easy for the business organisation to make strategies accordingly.

The present study, "Impact of Digital Marketing on Indian Firms" is an attempt in this direction. With this it becomes important to understand the perception of customers too, as they are one of the main assets of growth of any business. In this study, the perception of customers towards digital marketing is also studied. And the found results have shown that digital marketing is influencing customers in a great way and also in their decision making. Keeping all this in mind this study is carried out which can be a beneficial move for the business organisations in coming time. This whole thesis is further divided into six chapters as:

Chapter 1 deals with the introduction of the concept of digital marketing, evolution of digital marketing, modes of digital marketing, theories or models of digital marketing along with the framed objectives.

Chapter 2 deals with the literature review, in which the process of comprehensive literature review is carried out. With this the research gaps are also identified in this particular chapter.

Chapter 3 is devoted for the research methodology which is adopted to conduct the research in proper way. In this research design, sampling, statistical tools, framing of research instrument, hypothesis and limitations of the study is discussed.

Chapter 4 deals with the data analysis and results with discussion. In this all the results and interpretation are discussed in detail.

Chapter 5 attempts to summarise the whole research with the major findings, suggestions for the business organisations and the scope for further research.

Chapter 6 holds all the references, bibliography, web sources etc.

Keywords: Digital Marketing, Consumer Behaviour, Indian Firms

TABLE OF CONTENT

CHAPTER		TITLE	PAGE NO.

This chapter explores the concept of Digital Marketing with its evolution, growth and its comparison with traditional marketing, Consumer behaviour and online consumer behaviour with objectives and hypothesis.

1.1 Introduction

The number of internet users has risen dramatically in recent years. People nowadays spend the majority of their time online (566 million Internet Users as of December 2018 - Economic Times). Telecom companies like Reliance (R-Jio) are playing an important role in this continuous transformation. There are different factors which are regularly contributing in the growth of Internet like 4G services, Technological advancements. People are preferring to buy things online, having banking services online, and watch videos online. With the ever-expanding internet, take advantage of social media. As more and more things become digital, the corporate sector is likewise becoming more digital. India had between 480 and 570 million internet users in year 2018. And it is projected that by the year 2023, the internet users are expected to rise to 666.4 (Source: "Statista" - an online statistic, market research and business intelligence organisation).

Figure 1.1: Smartphone users in India

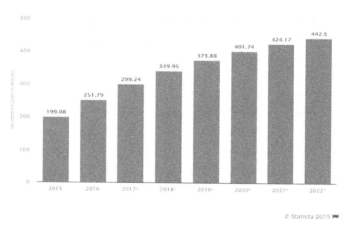

© Statista 2019

Source: Statista. (2019) Smartphone users in India. Available from: https://www.statista.com/ (Accessed: 14th May, 2019)

Business organisations are also utilising several digital channels for various processes within the organisation. In this regard, the increased use of smart phones is especially important. According to the figure 1.1 shown below, smart phone users are going to reach

1

approx. 442.5 million by 2022. (Source: "Statista" - an online statistic, market research and business intelligence portal). As a result, an increasing number of businesses are adopting digital media to promote their products or services. In this, social networking websites are playing a very crucial role. Business organizations have started relying on different digital channels such as e-mail marketing, search engine marketing and social media marketing etc to expand their digital presence. In this way, the internet is giving businesses a new opportunity, and it can be a very important and useful platform for their various marketing activities, such as spreading information, attracting new customers, retaining existing customers, and improving or maintaining relationships with existing customers through online CRM. With an ever-increasing rate of change, social media is radically altering the marketing environment. The consumer-company relationship is shifting as a result of social media. People are increasingly spending the majority of their time online. As a result, the business sector is turning away from traditional marketing and toward digital marketing. They are now promoting or advertising their products and services through digital marketing channels.

1.1.1 Digital Marketing Statistics in India

By the financial year 2024, this was expected to rise to roughly 539 billion rupees, demonstrating a significant increase in the industry area. (Statista)

Figure 1.2: Market Size of India's Digital Advertising (FY 2011-2024)

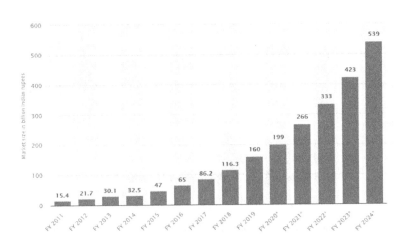

Source: Statista. (2019) Market Size of India's Digital Advertising. Available from: https://www.statista.com/ (Accessed: 25th June, 2019)

2

As per the report of IAMAI-Kantar ICUBE 2020 research published in Economic Times, in the next five years, the active Internet users in India is predicted to rise by 45 percent and will be reaching approx. 900 million by 2025, which were roughly 622 million in 2020. (Suginraj, 2017) with the reference of International Journal of Advance Research Foundation, has explained that India has been experiencing a golden time of digital marketing growth since 2013 and the trend is expected to continue at least through 2020.

As per a report of Statista (2020), there will be over 700 million internet users in India in the year 2020, and this is goint to rise approx. 974 million users, which will indiacte a large market for internet services. In fact, India was listed as the world's second-largest internet market in 2019, trailing only China. The number of internet users is expected to rise in both urban and rural areas, showing a dynamic increase in internet access.

Figure 1.3: Number of Internet Users in India

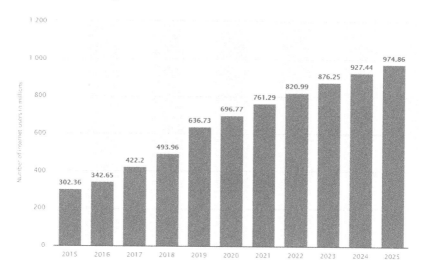

Source: Statista. (2021) Number of Internet Users in India. Available from: https://www.statista.com/ (Accessed: 28th April, 2021)

The vast majority of internet users in the country use their mobile phones to access the internet. Across the country, the number of smartphone users was roughly equal to the number of internet users. Some of the causes leading to India's mobile heavy internet access include the low cost of mobile data, a growing smartphone user base, and the utilitarian value of smartphones compared to desktops and tablets. Despite the country's enormous number of internet users, internet penetration levels took longer to catch up. At

3

the same time, women in India have far fewer internet users than men, and this disparity is even more pronounced in rural areas. Similarly, due to a lack of internet literacy and technological know-how, internet usage among older persons in the country is lower.

India's digital footprint has enormous capacity to develop if underprivileged populations, such as women, the elderly, and rural residents are encouraged to use the internet.

1.1.2 Industry-wise Adoption of Digital Marketing or Advertising in India

The worldwide usage of digital marketing is also showing an impact of the same in Indian Market too. Business organisations are spending a lot on the digital advertisements. Different industries are making use of digital marketing as per their needs or requirement. Industry wise share of digital ad spending is displayed in the chart below.

Figure 1.4: Industry-wise Spending on Digital Advertising

© Statista 2021

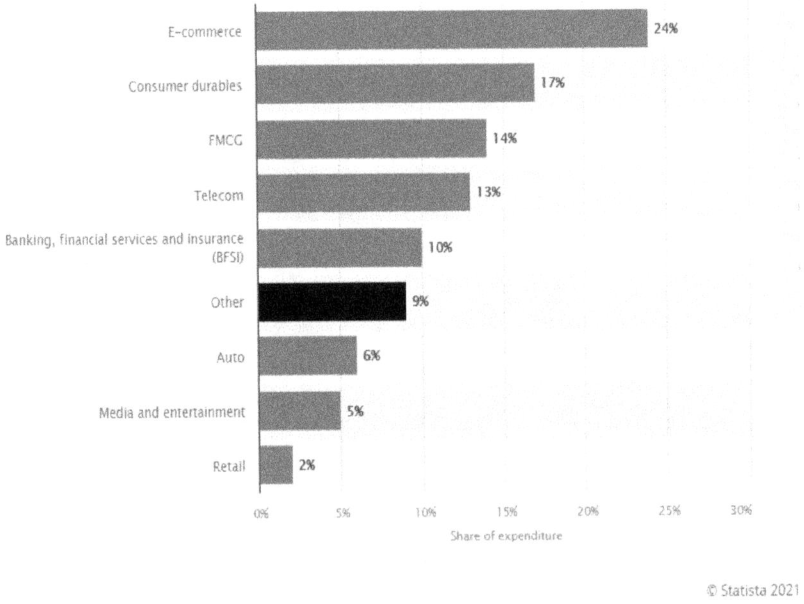

Source: Statista. (2021) Industry-wise Spending on Digital Advertising. Available from: https://www.statista.com/ (Accessed: 18th April, 2021)

From the above chart, it is very much cleared that usage of digital marketing is different from industry to industry. There are lots of variations in the shares of digital ad spending in this.

4

In the chart it is mentioned that E-Commerce with 24% of share is making the most use of digital advertisements followed by Consumer durables (17%), FMCG (14%) and least by retail (2%). From the chart it is cleared that business organisations are spending huge amount on the digital advertisements.

1.2 Marketing

Marketing is the activity, collection of institutions, and procedures for producing, communicating, delivering, and exchanging offerings that have value for customers, clients, partners, and society at large, according to the American Marketing Association (2013). Marketing is also defined as the process of identifying market/customer requirements and demands and meeting them profitably through an exchange process, or Marketing is the process of satisfying the needs and wants of customers through an exchange process (Philip Kotler).

1.2.1 Marketing Process

There is a marketing process that contains the following standard steps:

Figure 1.5: Marketing Process

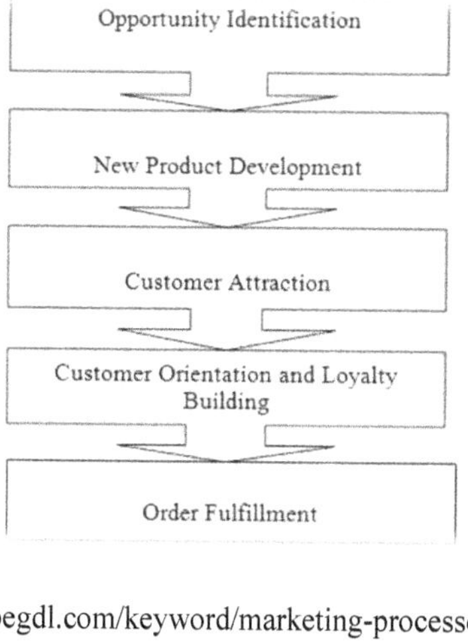

Opportunity Identification

New Product Development

Customer Attraction

Customer Orientation and Loyalty Building

Order Fulfillment

Source: http://canacopegdl.com/keyword/marketing-processes.html: accessed on 26/05/2019

1. Opportunity Identification: The first phase in the marketing process is to identify opportunities, such as what are the various market opportunities for a specific product or service, or what is the need or desire of customers for a specific product or service. This is the process of analysing a market or a set of clients.

2. New Product Development: This is the second and most crucial step in the marketing process. New product development begins at this point. This step builds on the findings of the first stage of the marketing process, which is opportunity identification.

3. Customer Attraction: The third step of the marketing process involves attracting people to a newly established product or service using various means or methods, such as advertising, branding, and promotion.

4. Customer Orientation and Loyalty Building: The fourth and most important stage of the marketing process is customer orientation and loyalty building. This stage entails enhancing the organization's goodwill and reputation, which aids in the retention of existing consumers as well as the acquisition of new ones.

5. Order fulfilment: This is the final step in the marketing process. The order is fulfilled in this procedure by meeting all of the clients' expectations, needs, wishes, and criteria.

After making a discussion on marking process, in the following sub-sections information is given on traditional marketing and modern marketing.

1.2.2 Traditional Marketing

Traditional Marketing is described as the marketing process in which commercials, promotions, and marketing are conducted in a traditional manner. These marketing tactics have been used for decades to promote, advertise, and educate customers.

Traditional Marketing Include

- Billboards
- Advertisements on TV and Radio
- Marketing through pamphlets, brochures, and other printed materials.
- Direct Mail Promotions (Fliers, Cards, Letters, Post Cards etc.)
- Magazines and newsletters
- Broadcast
- Using the telephone
- Door to Door and so on.

Traditional Marketing is basically the base of process of different promotional activities.

These were the promotional and advertisement tools used to market products or services, but as time has passed and technology has taken over, the concept of digital marketing has emerged. For various marketing activities, businesses began to use modern marketing's promotional and advertisement tools.

1.2.3 Modern Marketing

Modern Marketing is described as the marketing process in which commercials, promotions, and marketing are conducted in a modern manner. These marketing tactics are most in trend now and reducing the dominance of traditional approach of marketing.

Modern Marketing Include

- Societal Marketing
- Green marketing
- Relationship marketing
- Service marketing
- Digital marketing

It very important to give proper weightage to traditional as well as modern marketing. But, in recent years, we have seen orientation of many organizations had shifted to modern marketing because of the need of hour. Their marketing plans, budget, strategies and activities are directed by modern marketing. From the above-mentioned types of Modern Marketing, Digital Marketing is becoming the most important need of hour because of its efficiency and effectiveness. Digital Marketing is discussed in the next section.

1.3 Digital Marketing

As many people refer to it in different ways, the term "digital marketing" is used differently by everyone. It's also known as E-Marketing, Online Marketing, and Internet Marketing. Despite the fact that all of these phrases are connected in some way, there is a distinction between them (Rowan, 2002). Internet marketing is described as the use of the internet to promote and advertise goods and services. (Hanson and Kalyanam, 2007). Electronic marketing is the name given to e-marketing. Promotion and advertisement of items and services can be done using digital technology and a live internet connection (Hoge, 1993).

Digital marketing simply refers to the digital marketing of various products and services, as well as the use of various IT technologies and techniques for product and service advertisement and promotion. It's a new and effective technique to market products. It's a very different procedure than typical marketing. The practise of establishing and maintaining a relationship with clients through electronic media and various online activities is referred to as digital marketing. It covers a variety of methods for digitally engaging with audiences and generating leads and conversions for our organisation. Digital marketing is a dynamic process, unlike traditional marketing, in that it is constantly changing (Wymbs, 2011). We can measure the facts, numbers, and data in digital marketing, which makes it effective. It minimises the number of frantic door-to-door actions. It's also a cost-effective and convenient way to interact with people without bothering them.

The promotion of products or brands through one or more forms of electronic media is known as digital marketing. Digital marketing is also known as "online marketing," "internet marketing," or "web marketing." (Shirisha, 2018). The Chartered Institute of Marketing (2015) defines digital marketing as the management process responsible for identifying, anticipating, and profitably satisfying customer requirements. Smarter Insights (2000) defines Digital Marketing as "achieving marketing objectives through the use of digital technologies." As the world becomes more digital, the scope of digital marketing expands. This is because people believe it is a simple, convenient, and effective way to find out information. There is a growing demand for experts who can deal with issues related to electronic media.

Nowadays, everyone uses a mobile phone, particularly a smart phone. The industry is expanding on a daily basis, and the scope of digital marketing is expanding as well. The main point is that traditional marketing does not allow us to be everywhere, whereas digital marketing (via the internet and electronic media) allows us to be everywhere, at anytime, anywhere in the world. Essentially, digital marketing is a new approach to understanding customer behaviour and approaches.

1.3.1 Tools and Techniques of Digital Marketing

Digital Marketing is a collection of various tools and techniques that allow us to explore things in greater depth.

- SEO (Search Engine Optimization)
- SMO (Social Media Optimization)
- SMM (Social Media Marketing)
- SEM (Search Engine Marketing)
- Affiliate Marketing
- E-mail Marketing

8

- Content Marketing
- App Store Optimization (ASO)

1.3.1.1 Search Engine Optimization (SEO)

The process of optimising online content so that it appears as a top result in search engines such as Google, Bing, and Yahoo. It is the process of increasing a website's visibility in search results through the use of natural links. SEO is also referred to as Organic Search Results.

There are two types of SEO:

a. On Page SEO

b. Off Page SEO

a. On Page Optimization

On Page Optimization is defined as the type of SEO in which the optimized result is directly reflected on the website. On Page Optimization is one of the important techniques of SEO which is one of the main domain or mode of digital marketing.

Following Techniques are used for On Page Optimization:

- Keyword Research
- Title Tag Optimization
- Meta Tag Optimization
- Heading Tag Optimization
- URL Optimization and Rewriting
- Image Optimization
- Sitemap Creation (XML, HTML, ROBOT.txt)
- Content Optimization

Keyword Research

A keyword is simply a word with a specific meaning and value. Keyword research is the process of searching for and identifying keywords for use in an advertisement campaign or for any other search purpose. Keyword research can help you find the right search terms to help your content rank higher on search engines like Google.

It is a fundamental aspect of Search Engine Optimization (SEOS. Headings primarily assist search engines and readers in comprehending and reading the text.

Title Tag Optimization

A title tag is an HTML (Hyper Text Mark-up Language) component/element that defines or specifies the title of a web page. These tags are essentially shown or displayed on Search Engine Results Pages (SERPs) and can be clicked to provide the desired result. These assist search engines in obtaining detail or information about a web page. The title tags are typically placed on one of three platforms: Search Engine Results Pages (SERPs), Social Networks, and Web Browsers (MoZ).

Meta Tag Optimization

Meta tags are non-displayable, or hidden HTML tags that provide information about the webpage and indexing of the webpage (Henshaw, 1999; Henshaw and Valauskas, 2001). Meta tags are used to provide information and details about the content of a specific webpage or website. Meta tag optimization is required to ensure effective search results.

Heading Tag Optimization

Heading tag optimization is a search engine optimization (SEO) technique used to ensure a high-ranking on search engine results pages (SERP). Headings tags are the titles of posts that are published on a website.

Keywords play an important role in optimising a webpage's headings. Effective optimization of headings leads to effective Search Engine Optimization (SEO) results (SEO Yoast).

URL Optimization and Rewriting

A URL is a webpage address or web address that is used to locate a web page on the internet. Humans can easily read URL text, which allows computers to communicate with web servers (MoZ).

It is critical to improve or optimise the URL structure so that the reader and search engines can easily identify it. It should consist of both effective keywords and easily readable text. It should not be too long and should be free of superfluous words or characters.

Image Optimization

Images are a primary requirement for any article, advertisement, or post. Images, in essence, bring any post, article, or advertisement to life. It also helps to improve the SEO of any website. Images, when used effectively or correctly, can assist users or readers in easily understanding the content or post. Images enhance the appeal of articles, advertisements, and posts (SEO Yoast). The image should be responsive, with appropriate scaling, a size that is neither too large nor too small, and an alt tag and caption.

Sitemap Creation (XML, HTML, ROBOT.txt)

Creating a sitemap is important and required for website optimization. It is required for the best SEO results. Sitemaps provide all of the information about a website or webpage that search engines require. There are numerous tools available for creating sitemaps for various webpages or websites.

Content Optimization

As the name implies, content optimization is the process of "optimising the content." Content optimization entails writing content in such a way that it reaches a large audience, creates a good reach, and aids in lead generation. Content optimization includes a variety of processes such as text optimization, image optimization, meta tag description optimization, and so on. Content marketing is considered as one of the important digital marketing modes because this is getting more in trends nowadays.

b. Off Page Optimization

Off Page Optimization is a type of SEO in which the optimised result appears outside of the website, on other modes where we must create back links.

Techniques used for Off Page Optimization:

- Search Engine Submission
- Directory Submission
- Article Creation and Submission
- Blog Creation and Blog Submission
- Blog Commenting

Search Engine Submission

It is defined as the process getting the submission of the websites or webpages in the search engines. When the websites are listed in a particular search engine of your choice or need, this process is known as Search Engine Submission. It is also known as Search Engine Registration. Listing of websites on Search Engines, doesn't ensure the rank of your page on Search Engine Results Page (SERP), it simply means that it's in the knowledge of

11

search engines that this particular webpage exists. It is one of the main techniques of Off Page Optimization.

Directory Submission

This is one of the activities of Off Page Optimization. There are different kinds web directories available on the web. The process of the directory submission is to submit, register or list the webpages or websites on the respective web directory of your particular field.

Article Creation and Submission

Article Creation and Submission comes under the important techniques of Off Page Optimization. In this the article created or written by you will be submitted to the third-party websites or portals which are related to the same field for which the article has been written. There are different article submission directories related to different fields available on web in which the articles can be submitted for the promotion or branding of your business.

Blog Creation and Blog Submission

Blog Creation and Blog Submission is basically a similar kind of activity of Off Page Optimization, which is defined as process of submission of written blog which could be of any form in the particular blog site of your niche. Blog category could be different as per the need and requirement of the individual with respect to their niche or business.

Blog Commenting

Blog Commenting is defined as the technique in which you as an expert or the known of a particular field can comment your views on a particular field or subject matter. It is basically a cordial relation between Bloggers, Blog, and Blog Readers. Through this any individual can share their thoughts and knowledge with others through the written discussion on the blogs. Blog commenting is considered as one of the main aspect of Off Page Optimization.

1.3.1.2 Social Media Optimization (SMO)

Social Media Optimization is defined as the process of optimizing the content and components of the social media as per the requirement of every individual. The use of social media networks for managing and growing the content or message of any business organisation or individual online is known as Social Media Optimization. It is one of the greatest digital marketing strategies as it is used to enhance the reach, awareness of new product or services and connect with customers on different social media channels. Customization of the content on the social media channels is also one of the main things in Social Media Optimization. In this different social media management tools can be used to manage the content or different other activities on Social Media Channels. Few of the tools are:

- Loomly
- Agorapulse
- PromoRepublic
- Hootsuit
- Buffer
- Sprout Social etc.

1.3.1.3 Social Media Marketing (SMM)

Social Media Marketing is the process of identifying market needs and profitably meeting them through the use of various social media platforms. Facebook Marketing, Instagram Marketing, LinkedIn Marketing, Whatsapp Marketing, and other forms of Social Media Marketing exist. Social media enables businesses to integrate and communicate with their customers while also providing platforms for customers to communicate with one another around the world. (Faulds and Mangold, 2009). (Bajpai, 2012) explained in their study about the different tools of social media marketing as:

- ✓ Automation
- ✓ Social Media
- ✓ Social Aggregation
- ✓ Social Media Monitoring
- ✓ Social Bookmarking and Tagging
- ✓ Social Analytics and Reporting
- ✓ Blog Marketing etc.

Social Networking Sites (SNS): As the information and technology (IT) sectors continue to grow and develop, everyone now has access to all communication and information exchange channels. Social networking sites (SNS) are one of the most common ways for people to communicate and share or discuss various types of information and issues. Social networking sites provide a platform for all users to interact, share information, and have global discussions. Social networking sites basically function as a web-based service that allows individuals to create profiles, add connections from all over the world, and share things based on their preferences.

The interface and customization of various social networking sites can differ and be customised according to their terms and conditions.

Social Networking Sites are the fastest growing online domain, connecting millions of users worldwide. Social networking sites such as Facebook, Twitter, Instagram, LinkedIn, Whatsapp, WeChat, Tumblr, and others provide excellent platforms for people all over the world to interact and discuss issues.

The popularity of these social networking sites is rapidly increasing. These social networking sites have become an essential part of every person's life. As the majority of the world's population increasingly uses social networking sites, business organisations are shifting their focus to these sites. On these sites, they have begun to implement their marketing and promotional strategies and tactics. These are assisting them in effectively targeting the right audience at the right time and place with minimal effort. These sites are becoming an essential component of business organisations.

As a result, effective management of these sites is critical for any business organisation. The importance of social networking sites in business is rapidly increasing. Because more and more people are joining social networking sites at breakneck speed, business organisations are eager to make use of these sites as well. Businesses are capitalising on this brisk segment of cutting-edge technology. A large number of businesses are using these sites as a tool to build strong relationships with their customers and employees. Social networking sites are becoming technological innovations for businesses that cannot be overlooked.

Evolution of social networking sites

Social networking sites began in the early 1990s as an idea. classmates.com was the first social networking service, launched in 1995. This website was dedicated to education, higher education, employment, and the military. Bolt.com, the second social networking site, was created in 1996. Sixdegrees.com and Asian Avenue were the first two social networking sites to be founded in 1997. These were the websites that offered the option of creating profiles. Since then, various websites have emerged, each with its own set of features and tools. LinkedIn was created in 2003 for those who work in the business or professional world. Facebook and Orkut were both started in 2004. Orkut did not last much longer, but Facebook now has a massive global presence.

Features of social networking sites

Different technical and non-technical aspects can be found on social networking platforms. There are various features such as profile visibility, profile/display images, friends list, follower list, and likings. Name, demographic information, addresses, age, gender, location, and date of birth are all included in the profile. Other capabilities include photo and video sharing, blogging, wishes, and article submissions, among others. Many social networking sites also offer features such as private messaging or secret conversations to protect their users' privacy.

Many of the websites also have features that are tailored to commercial organisations. These business-oriented qualities assist businesses in working effectively and efficiently to reach their objectives with the least amount of investment and maximum output. Artificial Intelligence is a concept used in social networking sites to make them more interesting and dynamic.

Motive of Social Networking Sites

For Consumers: While everyone's reasons for utilising social networking sites are varied, most individuals use them to connect with their relatives and friends around the world. Other uses include photo sharing, video sharing, music listening, game playing, language learning, dating, talent search, social engagement, and education

For Business Organisations: The motivations for using social networking sites by businesses are several. Giving information, developing a brand image, and sharing facts or information about products and services are some of the main motivations for these for businesses. These sites are also being used by businesses as marketing and promotional tools in order to establish a brand image.

Management of Social Networking Sites

It's one thing to use social networking sites. However, one of the key challenges is the administration of these locations. It is critical to properly maintain and manage the website. What should you share, when should you share it, where should you share it, and with whom should you share it? The optimization of content and interface plays a critical part in site management as a result of this. What's the state of your website? Is the interface user-friendly? Is the content attractive and well-optimized? These are only a handful of the issues that a social networking site's management and maintenance entails.

Applications of Social Networking Sites in Different Sectors

As the world becomes more digital and everyone adapts to technology and innovation, social networking sites are being used by businesses of all sizes to build and grow their businesses. For every company organisation, these sites are becoming a necessity. These websites serve a variety of objectives for businesses, including advertising, marketing, promotions, recruitment, and selection.

As a result, the number of people using these sites is growing in each industry. The usage of social media has also been proven to minimise the cost of marketing, operations, and various promotional campaigns and activities. As a result, SNS can be stated to play a role in an organization's financial health.

Impacts of Social Networking Sites

According to previous research, social networking sites have a favourable impact on corporate organisations. Social networking platforms are becoming increasingly crucial in the development and expansion of businesses. People's interactions, connections, and thinking have all changed as a result of social networking sites. People are coming together thanks to social networking services, which are fostering a healthy relationship between consumers and businesses.

These websites assist businesses with branding and other aspects of their operations. These websites aid businesses in the creation of various marketing campaigns, the running of adverts, and the execution of various promotional activities, all while lowering the costs connected with various services and operations. Traditional marketing and promotion methods are no longer effective, and online marketing strategies are becoming popular. These sites are fundamentally transforming the business landscape, and they are quickly becoming a necessity for every firm.

Benefits of Social Networking Sites

Everyone requires a network in order to communicate with their family, friends, and other acquaintances. However, due to a hectic lifestyle and a lack of time, people are unable to meet everyone in person. Social networking platforms provide a solution to this problem. We may now digitally meet or connect with anyone, wherever in the globe.

There are numerous advantages to using social networking sites for everyone, including:

- Bring people together
- Allow everyone to exchange their thoughts, stories, and other information.
- Assisting businesses with various operations and tasks.
- Providing opportunities to meet people from all over the world.
- The operational costs of these sites are being reduced.
- Helpful in reaching a larger audience.
- Bring people together who share a common interest.
- Helpful in enhancing the brand awareness etc.

These are some of the most important advantages or benefits of using social media platforms for individuals and organisations.

Social networking sites are now playing an increasingly important part in the operations and activities of businesses. Workplace productivity is also influenced by social networking sites. Because they are cost effective, labour saving, and other factors, social networking sites are playing an increasingly important role in corporate development. These are the platforms for large-scale engagements that provide businesses with unrivalled prospects.

It is becoming increasingly crucial for businesses to have a presence on these platforms. One of the key concerns is not only the presence of these sites, but also their administration and maintenance. What should I share, where should I share it, and when should I share it? These are some of the most important considerations in social networking site management and upkeep. In the field of marketing and promotional operations, social networking sites are proving to be a major thing. As a result, businesses and business organisations are adjusting to accept new trends. These websites serve as forums for businesses to market and promote themselves. In the selling of products and services, advertisements are extremely significant. This is why social networking sites are becoming increasingly important for business growth and expansion. Interconnectivity and interaction are being facilitated by recent breakthroughs and innovations in the sphere of the internet. Both business organisations and consumers benefit from these healthy interactions. Consumer purchasing inclinations are also being influenced by social networking sites that provide value. Security, privacy, and other concerns or hazards are related with the usage of social networking services. However, as technology evolves and improves, these risks and difficulties are becoming less prevalent. Following an examination of several journal publications in this area, it was discovered that social networking sites have a significant impact on business and have a large future potential. As a result, the use and management of social networking sites is a critical problem and necessity of the hour for businesses.

1.3.1.4 Search Engine Marketing (SEM)

This is the process of promoting and advertising various products or services using various search engines. It is a sort of marketing that is paid. We must pay search engines for our firms' ads and promotional efforts. Google AdWords, Bing Ads, and other kinds of Search Engine Marketing exist. On search engines, several types of ad campaigns can be built, such as text ad campaigns, display ad campaigns, shopping ad campaigns, video ad campaigns, and so on.

Search Engine Marketing is basically following the same thing like SEO except it's one of the main and different features i.e., it is a paid form of online marketing technique which increase the visibility of the websites on Search Engine Results Page (SERP). It is also known as Pay Per Click (PPC).

Why SEM is Important?

As the business are getting online day by day, business organisations are getting more inclined towards online marketing and because this is one of the important techniques of digital marketing companies are focusing more on this. Search engine marketing has become a critical online marketing approach for expanding a company's reach, as an increasing number of people study and shop for products online.

In fact, the vast majority of new visitors to a website arrive from a search engine query. Advertisers only pay for impressions that result in visitors in search engine marketing, making it a cost-effective option for a company to spend its marketing budget. As an added advantage, each visitor helps to boost the website's organic search results rankings. When compared to other sites such as social media, where users are not intentionally searching for something, customers entering search queries with the aim of discovering commercial information are in an optimal state of mind to make a purchase. Consumers are most receptive to fresh information when they are exposed to search marketing. PPC advertising is non-intrusive and does not disrupt their tasks, unlike the majority of internet advertising. SEM provides immediate results. It is, without a doubt, the quickest technique to get people to visit a website.

1.3.1.5 Affiliate Marketing

Affiliate Marketing is defined as Affiliate marketing is the process of earning money (commissions) every time you promote a company's products or services and drive a sale. You only get paid every time you drive a sale, just like a commission-only sales representative.

Affiliate marketing is a type of marketing in which other firms' products and services are advertised on well-known websites such as blogs, websites, and social media channels. For which we are paid a commission for promoting and advertising that product or service.

Affiliate marketing is a type of advertising in which a firm pays third-party publishers to send traffic or leads to its products and services. Affiliates are third-party publications who are paid a commission to create new methods to promote the firm.

Process of Affiliate Marketing

Process of Affiliate Marketing is explained below. The process is, Join the Affiliate Program, Promotion of that Program or Product and the last one is you will be paid for the promotion of that particular product or program.

Figure 1.6: Process of Affiliate Marketing

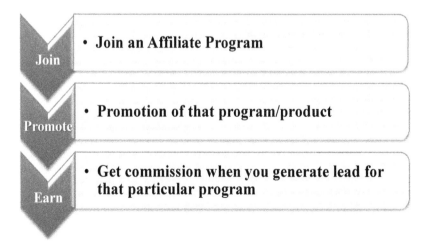

Source: Theoretical Process of Affiliate Marketing framed by Author

19

1.3.1.6 E-mail Marketing

Email marketing is the process of sending promotional emails to customers. New subscribers, active subscribers, inactive subscribers, and permanent clients are all possible. All email marketing campaigns are fully automated according to the current situation.

Types of Emails:

1. Promotional mails
2. Transactional mails
3. Birthday Wishes
4. Offers
5. Greeting mails etc.

Software like as mail chimp, active campaign, constant contact, send in blue, Hub Spot, and others are frequently used to send these emails.

Process of Email Marketing

- Define the audience
- Establish the goals and objectives
- Allow people to sign up
- Selection of type of Email Campaign
- Schedule Preparation
- Results Measurements

These are the general steps or we can say strategies to run a successful Email Marketing campaign.

1.3.1.7 App Store Optimization (ASO)

App Store Optimization is the art of increasing the visibility of an app in the Google Play or Apple App Stores. This strategy aims to increase a certain app's rating in the Google Android and Apple iOS play stores.

App Store Optimization (ASO), also known as App Store Marketing or Mobile App SEO, is a term used to describe the process of optimising an app for the app store.

ASO is primarily concerned with increasing the visibility of your apps within a search engine for app stores such as Google Play or Apple App Store. Other objectives, such as visitors to your web app and downloads, might be aided by increasing impressions.

The objectives and goals of App Store Optimization are:

- Expansion of brand exposure

- Positive feedbacks and reviews on apps
- Increment in the volume of reviews on apps
- Engagement of audience
- Diversifications of marketing channels associated

1.4 Digital Marketing Channels

Digital marketing channels are the means by which businesses carry out various digital marketing activities. Websites, blogs, emails, social networking websites, digital TVs, smart phones, and other sorts of current and in-demand digital marketing channels utilised by large and small businesses were listed by (Wertime and Fenwick 2011).

Figure 1.7: Digital Marketing Channels

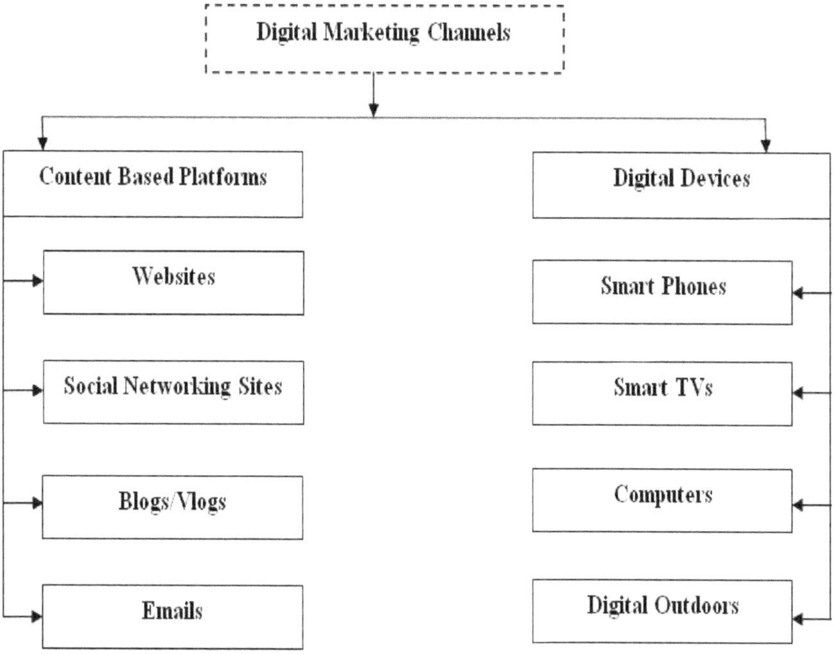

Source: (Wertime, K. and Fenwick, I, 2011). DigiMarketing: The essential guide to new media and digital marketing. Hoboken, NJ: John Wiley & Sons.

1.4.1 Content Based Platforms

Content based platforms are the platforms or the mediums which provide the different content to the audiences and readers. On these platforms or channels, the readers get plenty of content to read or interact.

Few of the digital marketing channels are:

- Websites – It can be a web page, or online portal
- Social Networking Sites – different social networking channels like Facebook, WhatsApp, Instagram etc.
- Blogs/Vlogs – A platform with written and displayed content and vlog is the video content platform like YouTube etc.
- Emails – Different emails official as well as promotional.

1.4.2 Digital Devices

Digital devices are those devices which are used to engage the audience for the online content. Online content can be accessed with the use of Digital Devices. Few of the digital devices are:

- Smartphones – one of the main and primary digital device used by maximum of the audiences.
- Smart Tvs – Presently most in trend which can be used for different type of purposes
- Computers – Computers or Laptops are also one of the main digital devices used by the users.
- Digital Outdoors – digital outdoors can be seen in different places nowadays showing digital ads. For example, in a football or cricket match we can see dynamic display ads on screens which keep on changing with time.

1.5 Advantages of Digital Marketing Over Traditional Marketing

Digital marketing has a number of advantages over traditional marketing.

- **Low Cost:** Digital marketing is a cost-effective method. When compared to traditional marketing, advertising items and services online is less expensive.
- **Real-Time Outcomes:** Digital marketing is a method for displaying real-time results. It is a real-time process; we begin receiving results immediately after the advertisement programme begins, such as tracking client replies, speedy resolution of queries, and so on, whereas traditional marketing requires us to wait for results because it is a sluggish process.
- **Brand Development:** The digital marketing method is the most efficient technique to establish a brand name in a short amount of time, whereas traditional marketing takes a long time. The reach to reach the largest possible audience is rising by utilising a variety of digital marketing methods (social media, Search Engine

Optimization, and Email Marketing) and campaigns. More people are influenced as a result of the use of these methods and initiatives.

- **Non-invasive:** Advertisements and promotional activities in newspapers and magazines are often bothersome since they are fixed, whereas online advertisements can be avoided at any moment.
- **Greater Exposure:** When compared to traditional marketing, digital marketing delivers more exposure in commercials and promotional activities because it has a global reach through the Internet and can target the correct audience at the right time and place.
- **Better Interaction:** When compared to traditional marketing, digital marketing engages or targets a larger audience through a variety of modules (such as social media engagement, search engine campaigns, and appealing email marketing strategies).
- **Faster Publicity:** When compared to traditional marketing, digital marketing is a faster means to publicise goods and services on a wide scale. This is being used extensively by businesses. They personalise products to meet the needs of their clients.
- **Easy Analytics:** When compared to traditional marketing, digital marketing efforts are simple and quick to analyse. Digital marketing can make use of analytical tools such as Google Search Console, Google Analytics, and others. This research is also assisting in the development of new marketing tactics at all levels.

1.6 Digital Marketing Process

The term "digital marketing process" is a fairly broad term that refers to a variety of digital marketing activities. As a result, Digital Marketing serves the needs of individuals through a variety of platforms and strategies. There are numerous tactics and processes to follow when it comes to digital marketing for each organisation.

Digital Marketing process constitutes of different steps which are:

- Determine Client Goals
- Develop Strategy
- Determine Solutions
- Execute
- Measure and Refine

Figure 1.8: General Process of Digital Marketing

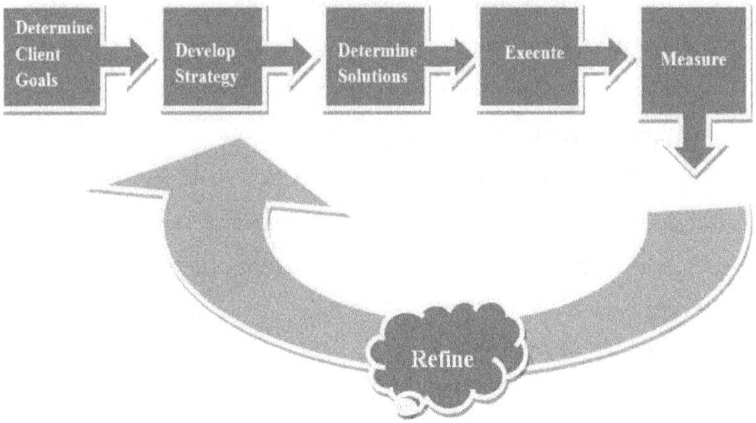

Source: Webclincher. (2019) Process of Digital Marketing. Available from
https://www.webclincher.com/digital-marketing-process/ (Accessed on 28th May, 2019)

1. **Determine Client Goals:** This is the first step of digital marketing process. The goals or objectives of clients are defined and determined in this perticular step.

2. **Develop Strategy:** This step is evolved around the development of different digital marketing strategies which will be suitable for digital marketing campaign

3. **Determine Solutions:** In this perticular step, the different solutions are determined which are required for the developed digital marketing startegies.

4. **Execute:** This step is to put all of the strategy-oriented solutions into action across various digital marketing campaigns. Individuals' requirements are met through the use of digital marketing channels such as social media platforms, search engines, and so on.

5. **Measure:** After the execution of strategies and solutions, the outcomes and results are measured. Measurement tools come in a variety of shapes and sizes.

6. **Refine:** The final but not least step entails fine-tuning all of the strategies and solutions in light of the expected outcomes and results. In this perticular step the refinement of all the activities are done which was involved in the process.

1.7 Model of Digital Marketing

5-S Model of Digital Marketing explain the benefits of digital marketing for the business organisations. It was given by Dave Chaffey.

The Model is further explained below with its main components.

24

Sell – Grow Sales

Sale is considered as the most important transaction that leads to make a decent profit and revenue.

Serve – Add Value

Values can be added by providing customers a platform where they can share their valuable feedbacks, have their queries, and can also post their complaints. This platform could be a web portal, web page or a website.

Figure 1.9: 5-S Model of Digital Marketing

Source: https://www.smartinsights.com/goal-setting-evaluation/goals-kpis/goals-for-your-digital-marketing/ on dated: 22/01/2021

Speak – Go closer to Customers

Not only sales, the communication can also be excelled with the use of online platforms with the engagement of customers in different events or activities online.

Save – Save Costs

It is also helpful in saving the cost of different promotional, advertisement activities as most of the service cost, printing costs, postage costs etc. can be reduced by the use of eMarketing.

Sizzle – Extend the brand value

The brand value can be excelled by sizzling. Effective and positive brand experience can create a huge advantage for the brands to grow more. This can also help in the engagement of audiences in a smooth way and that can create a positive impact on the customer base.

Table 1.1 explains the benefits of digital marketing for the business organisations and that is explained with the 5S model of Dave Chaffey.

Table 1.1: 5 Ss of Digital Marketing with Benefit Delivered

5S& Benefits of Digital Marketing	How benefit is delivered	Examples of Typical Objectives
Sell – Grow Sales	Benefit can be delivered by: • Selling online • Creating wider distribution channels • Lowering prices/discounts • Creating wider Product range in comparison with other channels	• Increase the sales of a particular product or service by 20 to 30% in a particular year. • Achieve a target of particular number in assigned period.
Serve – Add Value	It can be delivered by: • Giving customers some kind of extra benefits online • Informing properly about the particular product development • By answering all the feedbacks and reviews online	• Increase in the dialogue and interaction on online platforms • Conversion rate can be increased by some target values.
Speak – get closer to customers	It can be delivered by: • Creating to way communication or dialogue with customers • Enhancing web interactions through online forums and surveys and tracking the leads	• Customer survey of 1000 customers each month through emails or any other platforms • Increase in the customer database by tracking the conversions
Save – Save costs	It can be delivered by: • Online activities can reduce the staff • Online promotions and advertisements are cost effective as it saves the printing and paper cost and can easily be customised as required less efforts in installing.	• Can create multiple advertisements campaign by single budget plan • Email marketing can reduce the cost of direct marketing
Sizzle – Extend the brand online	It can be delivered by: • Providing fresh offers • Fresh propositions • Building new online experience through online communities	• Brand awareness can be increased • Audience reach can be increased • Brand favourability can be increased.

Source: Chaffey and Smith (2012)

1.8 Challenges in Adoption of Digital Marketing

As per different authors, there can be different types of barriers or challenges in the adoption of digital marketing or during the creation of digital marketing strategies. Some of the authors like (El-Gohary, Trueman and Fukukawa, 2009), (Leeflang *et al.*, 2014), (Ištvanić, Milić and Krpić, 2017) etc. have identified few challenges like management of the received data, government policies, lack of finance, identification of right tools and technology, training of staff, changing customers' behaviour etc.

Research by Smart Insight (2014), have investigated different challenges in managing digital marketing. The key areas are identified as:

1.8.1 Planning

It has found in the research that approx. 50% or half of the business organisations are lacking in the effective plan for adoption of digital marketing, and many organisations are not working as per plan.

1.8.2 Organisational Capabilities

It is also found in the conducted research that nearly 45% of the business organisations are doing good in this area but else are lacking in the organisational capabilities in terms of adopting digital marketing.

1.8.3 Integration of digital channels into marketing

Few of the companies are happy by their integration level of digital channels into marketing. There are some barriers identified in the case of integration i.e., Lacking in integrated plan and strategies, Unstructured teams, lacking in skills required in the integrated communications.

1.8.4 ROI Evaluation

A great proportion of business organisations were seeing a great opportunity in the adoption of digital marketing but they find it challenging to measure the Return on Investment (ROI) of the campaign and that could be a great area of concern for the managers. ROI is important in overall considerations also. As we have discussed different challenges or barriers in the adoption of digital marketing, now the main question or concern should be that how the business organisations can reduce or meet out these challenges successfully and effectively. For this there is a 7S model given or summarised by (Waterman et al, 1980) and developed by Mckinsey consultants (1980).

1.9 7-S Model of Mckinsey

7S model given or summarised by (Waterman et al, 1980) and developed by Mckinsey consultants (1980). To reduce the challenges and concerns in the adoption of digital marketing for business firms this 7-S was given.

Figure 1.10: Mckinsey's 7S Model of Digital Marketing

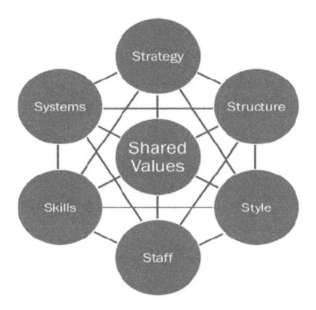

(Source: https://www.smartinsights.com/marketing-planning/marketing-models/mckinsey-7s-model/ accessed on date: 22/01/2021)

The above figure explains the Mckinsey's 7S framework which is used in digital marketing. In this the seven elements of the model are mentioned which are like: Strategy, Structure, Style, Staff, Skills, Systems and Shared Values. These elements contribute in the applications to different strategies of digital marketing which are helpful for the organisations to take decisions in the right favourable directions.

Econsultancy (2005) has summarised this and have focus on few of the strategic resource management issues where the consideration is required, which is explained in the table below:

Table 1.2 Mckinsey's 7 S Model of Digital Marketing

Elements of 7s Model	Application to digital marketing strategy	Key issues from practice and literature
Strategy	The role of digital marketing in supporting and influencing the strategy of the organisation.	To impact and aligning digital marketing strategy, the use of different techniques of digital marketing
Structure	In the support of digital marketing, the organisational structure can be modified and improved	<ul><li>Outsourcing vs Insourcing</li><li>Usage of steering groups and cross-functional teams</li><li>Digital marketing and ecommerce team's integration with other management</li></ul>
System	To support digital marketing, development of different specific information systems, procedures and processes	<ul><li>Content quality management</li><li>Planning of campaigns</li><li>Customer information management</li></ul>
Staff	To ensure the breakdown of staff as per the background and characteristics, e.g., department wise, Age and gender wise etc.	<ul><li>Outsourcing vs Insourcing</li><li>Retention and recruitment of the staff</li><li>Virtual working</li><li>Training and development of the staff</li></ul>
Style	Considering both the ways which are cultural style of the organisation as a whole, role of managers in achieving the organisational goals	Digital marketing team role in influencing strategy
Skills	Different distinctive capabilities of staff members with the specific skill set of the team members	<ul><li>Particular eMarketing approaches like SEM SEO SMM etc.</li><li>Skill set of staff in specific areas like supplier selection, project management etc.</li></ul>
Superordinate Goals	The digital marketing organisations' guiding concepts which are also a important part of shared values and culture. There may be the variation in the internal and external perception of these goals.	Improvement in the perception of importance and effectiveness amongst the digital marketing team members with their seniors or their staff they work with

Source: Econsultancy (2005) – Adapted from Dave Caffey – Digital Marketing Strategy and implementation – 6th Edition

1.10 Management of Digital Marketing

To understand the management of digital marketing in business, it becomes more important to understand few things about digital marketing like: what is involved in digital marketing? what are the different activities which are required for the purpose of digital marketing? how those activities or operations are related to different other marketing operations or activities? According to "Dave Chaffey" it is difficult to get the desired investment without the basic understanding of digital marketing in the firms.

As per some basic observations, there are few misconceptions of digital marketing like:

- We are making effective use of digital marketing because we have a website
- We are using digital marketing because we have a Facebook account

These misconceptions are narrowing the scope of digital marketing and things are getting confined to these misconceptions only. This is not good for the business firms as well as for the future of digital marketing scope.

"Dave Chaffey" has suggested that to understand the importance of digital marketing in future perspective in business, the one of the main things to consider is 'Audience Interaction'. For the management of digital marketing activities or operations effectively considering the audience, "Dave Chaffey" has given a 7D Model.

Figure 1.11: Dave Chaffey's 7D Model of Digital Marketing

Digital goals	Digital audiences	Digital devices	Digital platforms	Digital media	Digital data	Digital technology
Brand goals and strategy	Business-to-consumer	Smartphone	Facebook	Paid	Customer profiles	Software-as-a-Service
SMART comms objectives	Business-to-business	Tablet	Amazon	Owned	Customer behaviours	Martech including Marketing clouds
Always-on and campaign integration		Desktop	Microsoft	Earned	Customer value	Marketing automation
Digital transformation and disruption	Consumer-to-consumer	Smart speaker and in-home	Google	Websites and apps	Communications preferences	Artificial Intelligence
Business and revenue models (monetisation)	Target markets, segments and personas	Digital TV and Out-of-home signage	Apple	Search, social and email marketing	Big Data	Augmented and virtual reality
			Other sector-specific intermediaries	Content marketing and PR		

Source: www.davechaffey.com/digital-marketing-definitions/what-is-digital-marketing/

It becomes very important to understand the audience in an effective and right way, which is a very challenging task to do, because it is very difficult to understand the human behaviour.

Digital Goals

There could be different digital goals like:

- To review the aim or purpose of business organisations to achieve with the help of digital marketing
- To check how business organisations can compete effectively with the competitors by making use of digital marketing activities
- To focus on to create the SMART objectives.

Digital Audience

- To understand the different characteristics of the online audience
- Understanding the behaviour and preferences of the online audience to ensure the effective services for the target segement
- This will lead to increase better interaction and can have better engagements which will lead to better results in order to achieve the business goals

Digital Devices

This is one of the main aspects in the management of digital marketing in context of customer or audience.

- Because to interact with the online audience, business organisations need to take care of management of different digital devices like Smartphones, Laptops, Tablets SmartTvs etc.

Digital Platforms

- Digital devices need a platform to have access of the things. These platforms are known as digital platforms
- These could be through browsers and platforms could be social media channels like Facebook, Instagram etc., search engines, eCommerce websites or portals etc.

Digital Media

Digital media could be the part of digital platforms.

- These can be the paid, earned and owned media communication platforms.
- These interactions or commincations can be through email, search engines, messaging, social media channels.
- Personal apps or websites of business firms can be the example of owned digital media.

Digital Data

- Digital data is a kind of insight about the online audiences.
- Their interactions, profiles, needs or requirements
- The management of digital data is very crucial aspect in digital marketing management.

Digital Technology

- These are the different marketing tools and techniques business firms are using to create the interactive sessions or experiences.
- This could be through personal owned websites, apps or through different advertisement campaigns.

These are the 7Ds which were given by "Dave Chaffey" to manage the digital marketing by keeping the audience aspect in mind to achieve the business goals or objectives effectively.

In the above sections, we have discussed about the digital marketing and the role of digital marketing in business context. In the following section, we are discussing about the consumers' perception towards the digital marketing and online consumer behaviour

1.11 Consumer Behaviour

Consumer buying behaviour is basically the way in which consumers behave or react while purchasing a product or service. Consumers are considered as the king of market and it is important to understand the need and demand of consumers, (Pawar S.A and Naranje S, (2016) consumer buying behaviour is considered as the integral and important of market strategic planning. Understanding the consumer behaviour have become an essential competitive tool for business organisations. Consumer behaviours are the situations that may be finished with purchasing or not, (A. Koyluoglu S, et al, 2018). Consumer buying behaviour is the threshold of customer relationship management (CRM), (Sur M, 2017).

1.12 Online Consumer Behaviour

We know that domination of Internet and digital devices are increasing tremendously and customers are getting access to digital things with ease. This is creating a huge impact on behaviour of the consumers. Nowadays the consumers are thinking and making decision as per the content they find online over the internet. The reason behind this is that maximum of their time, they spend online. They are interacting, communicating online, getting their work done online, studying online. It becomes obvious to have a shift in the behaviour of consumers. This changed consumer behaviour is termed as "online consumer behaviour".

It is a kind of digital revolution which is creating this changing impact on consumers as well as the business organisations. Nowadays we can see maximum of the individuals are with the smartphones, tablet or laptops in their hands, which are permanently connected to internet and getting access of social media channels, online portals and email accounts (Fuciu, 2015). As per "(Close, 2012, pp. 11 – 12)", the concept of consumer behaviour has not changed that much but there are some improvements in terms of addition in online environment. In this era the consumer buying behaviour towards products or services is based on both the offline stores as well as online. Few studies like "(Dorley, 2010), (Cummins, 2014)" have discussed that interaction between online environment and consumer behaviour have increased to some extent.

When we talk about the consumer decision making process, according to (Kotler and Armstrong, 2008, p. 209; Catoiu and Teodorescu, 2004), the components of offline and online behaviour are same which are:

- Need Recognition
- Searching Information
- Evaluation of Alternatives
- Decision Making
- Post Purchase Behaviour

Online consumer behaviour also depends upon some factors like:

- Price
- Trust

- Convenience (Fuciu, 2015). These are very crucial in the context of online environment.

Virtual shopping and understanding of online consumer behaviour are becoming the need of hour for the business organisations. Business firms are taking these things on the priority basis and that is the actual demand of the present time because the condition of competitive virtual marketplace. Regular expansion and development of Internet gradually, creating a transformation of eCommerce into the mainstream activities of business (Constantinides, 2004).

1.12.1 Forces Influencing the Online Consumer Behaviour

As per the figure mentioned below which is adapted from (Constantinides, 2004), the first stage which is termed as the search stage. In this stage the audience will look for different reviews on products or services, comments of customers and the feedback and queries of the customers regarding a product or service.

Figure 1.12: Online Consumer Behaviour Framework

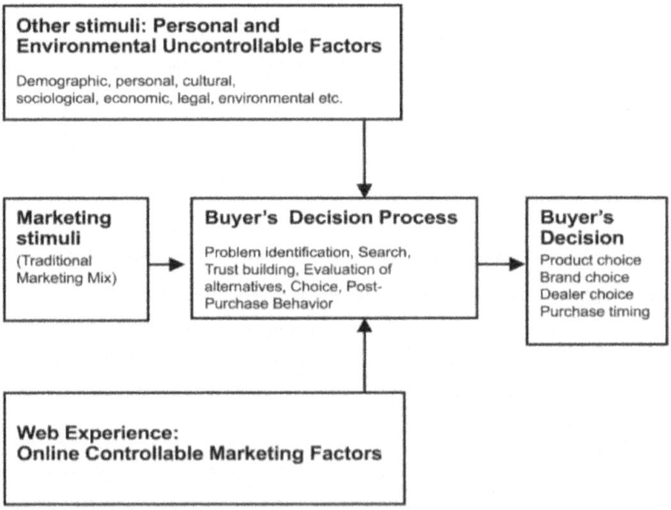

Source: Based on the P. Kotler's Framework (2003)

Audience will also come to know about the different brands and their offerings and decide which of the brand is fitting in their needs and expectations. They follow brands very closely and make their purchasing decisions according to that In this stage, important components could be:

34

- Well Optimised Website
- Well Structured Website
- Website Design and attractiveness
- Content etc.

Customers like first stage of this framework because of the characteristics of the different components involved, because they help customers in making a comprehensive and genuine comparison between different options.

In the next stage which is purchasing stage, the most important factors which help customers to select the product or decide the seller are:

- Product Assortment
- Sale Services
- Quality of information etc.

The next stage in this is the stage of post purchase behaviour. It becomes important after the stage of online purchasing. After purchasing the product, many a times customers have different kind of concerns regarding the product they have bought. These concerns might be regarding different aspects which are:

Change, Return, Replace etc. These are some of the important aspects of this stage which is post purchasing behaviour stage.

1.12.2 Factors of Online Consumer Behaviour

The different past studies have categorised the different factors of online consumer behaviour in different ways. Few have categorised them as:

- External Factors
- Internal Factors
- The Functional Motives
- Non-Functional Motives etc.

(Constantinides, 2004) explained these factors in the categories like:

- Functionality Factors
- Psychological Factors
- Content Factors

These are based on the usability, interactivity, trust, aesthetics and marketing mix etc. The filtering elements of these factors are:

- Security
- Privacy
- Trust and Trustworthiness

Customers generally make use of these three filtering factors to make the purchase choices, selection of design, product type and deciding the sellers etc.

1.13 Covid-19 and Digital Marketing

Before the outspread of the Covid-19 the business organizations and economies were growing with a great pace. But then by the end of year 2019, Corona Virus (Covid-19) has started causing its impact globally. This outspread was declared as a pandemic by World Health Organization (WHO). Covid-19 have impacted the business as well as the economic world disastrously (Ling, G.H.T., & Ho, C.M.C., 2020).

There were different corona virus outspreads in the past in different countries, but the infection and death rate of Covid-19 was tremendously higher as compared to other (Peeri et al., 2020)(Liu *et al.*, 2020). Covid-19 have changed all the global activities drastically. In the history of mankind this is one of the drastic outspread. All the developed, developing and underdeveloped economies got affected by this pandemic as whole world was under lockdown. This outspread has created an unrest in the business world also. Many people have lost their jobs due to different reasons.

For the business organizations it was difficult to survive as the market and all the business activities were halted or minimized. There was the dire need of strategy shift for business organizations, because the strategies they were following to strive were no longer feasible. It was very difficult for the business organizations to create a real ambiance of their products or services for consumers due to lockdown or social distancing and other restrictions. Covid-19 have constrained business organizations to shift online for the advertisement and promotion of their products or services. So that they can create a strong customer base even after the lockdown situations.

1.14 Emergence of the Problem

It is quite evident from the discussion made in the previous sections that Digital Marketing is a new basic in the corporate world. It is the most post popular and important marketing trend in the present time. As this is becoming the major aspect in marketing, it becomes important to study the impacts of digital marketing on firms as well as what are the perception and views of customers about digital marketing. But if we have a look on the secondary data or on existing literature, there are very few studies available which have covered this important aspect of marketing i.e., Digital Marketing. Hence the following raised research questions need to be answered or examined.

What are the favorable factors towards adoption of digital marketing? How government and other forces playing a significant role in the adoption of digital marketing? What is the cost of campaign setup, infrastructure, and other basic requirements and facilities? What benefits business organizations are getting after the adoption of digital marketing? Which factors encourage business organizations most towards the adoption of digital marketing? What strategies are being used by business organizations to reap the maximum benefits of digital marketing? What are the challenges and benefits business organizations are facing after the adoption of the same? How digital marketing is impacting their sales, marketing share, customer relationship management, etc? What are the perceptions of consumers toward digital marketing? How do they perceive digital marketing? Are they influenced by digital marketing or not? Which form of digital marketing appeals most to them? How social media presence is important for business organizations? Businesses are getting benefits from their presence on social media channels or not. Which social media channel is more effective for business organizations like (Facebook, Twitter, Instagram, Tumblr, Whatsapp etc.)? What will be the impact of upcoming technologies like 5G, artificial intelligence, machine learning etc. on digital marketing adoption?

The present study is focused on the different impacts of digital marketing on firms and to know the perception of consumers towards digital marketing. This study will further help different business firms to make effective and efficient strategies for their business to get the maximum of the competitive advantage.

1.15 Objectives of the study

1. To study the emergence of digital marketing in the Indian scenario. (YOY secondary data analysis).
2. To identify the factors that motivates adoption of digital marketing.
3. To identify the challenges or problems faced by the firms during adoption or implimentation.

4. To measure the impact of digital marketing on the sales of business firms.

5. To identify the most effective mode of digital marketing that influences firms.

6. To analyze customers' perception towards digital marketing.

Digital marketing gives all businesses, large and small, the same opportunity. Previously, only affluent companies could advertise their products and services due to the high cost of traditional marketing and advertising compared to digital marketing. Digital marketing is significantly affecting and altering the entire company landscape. Less money spent yields excellent benefits. Businesses are obtaining the most output for the least amount of money. Use of digital technologies and Internet helping in the creation of advertisements which are dynamic in nature and penetrating worldwide.

Literature review is basically a summary of the research topics or the studies which are published previously. It gives the general idea of the research carried earlier. The literature can be reviewed through scholarly articles, books, research papers and other resources which are relevant to a particular research field. Literature review provides general direction for research to be carried out by highlighting the aspects in which research has been carried out earlier. These are the secondary resources of past research. It is basically a kind of handy guide of past research information. This chapter basically deals with review of literature dealing in digital marketing to explore the existing research gap and research perspectives associated with digital marketing.

The present study focuses on the evolving research topic i.e. digital marketing and impact of digital marketing on the corporate sector. The impact of digital marketing plays an important and significant role for the business organizations. The following related literature is reviewed to fulfil or to meet the objectives of the study. For this purpose, different research articles, books, journal, research papers are analysed and reviewed.

Wind & Mahajan (2002) discussed about the digital revolution, which has totally changed the scenario of business by offering different benefits to customers (Price transparency, easy excess etc.) and to companies (cost effective, easy customization and vast reach etc). They explained that the digital technology has changed the way customers relate themselves with products and markets. Consumers are becoming the cyber consumer. They concluded that as digital revolution is taking place; businesses are focusing more on digital technologies to survive in the competitive market.

Verma & Munjal (2003) identified the major factors in making a brand choice decision namely quality, price, availability, packaging and advertisement. The brand loyalty is a function of woman behavioural and cognitive patterns of a customer. Although the age at demographic variables affects behavioural and cognitive patterns of the customers there is hardly a room for other demographic characteristics of gender and marital status.

Ganeshmoorthy, Radhakrishnan & Bhuneshwari (2003) has studied the brand loyalty of the products and the influence of mass Media, in rural markets. The study revealed that mass Media, had a significant role in the sales promotion of the select products. Besides it has been added that it is the quality of the product that is given the preference. The factors such as price and availability are merely second thought.

Naidu (2004) in his study an attempt had been made to analyse the awareness level of rural consumers. It was found from the study that awareness of the rural consumers about the consumer movements were qualitative in character and cannot be measured directly in quantitative terms. There is no fixed value or scale which will help to measure the awareness. But the awareness had been studied with the help of their responses to various questionnaires relating to consumer movements, cosmetics, banking services, drugs, food products, tooth pastes and hair oil. Awareness levels were higher in the above said segments in Ranga Reddy of Andhra Pradesh.

Madhavi and Kumar (2006) In their study pointed out that most of the rural woman consumers are influenced by quality of the product. So, the FMCG Companies should strictly adhere to the quality standards. Price is the second factor that influences the purchase of the product in most cases and hence the product should be reasonably priced. They concluded that FMCG companies could significantly increase the market share by extending attention of rural areas. More generic product with different advertisement campaigns surely attracts non-users.

Raj (2007) This paper covers the attractions for the FMCG marketers to go to rural and the urban markets and uses a suitable marketing strategy with the suitable example of companies and their experience in going rural. Thus, the rural marketing has been growing steadily over the years and is now bigger than the urban market for FMCG. Globally, the FMCG sector has been successful in selling products to the lower- and middle-income groups and the same is true in India. Over 70% of sales is made to middle class households today and over 50% of the middle class is in rural India. But the rural penetration rates are low. This presents a tremendous opportunity for makers of branded products who can convert consumers to buy branded products. The marketers need to develop different strategies to treat the rural consumers since they are economically, socially and psychographically different from each other.

Ghosh (2007) identified key challenges for FMCG companies who are penetrating the rural markets, which include infrastructure issues like poor distribution system, improper logistics and the fragmented rural market, given the heterogeneity of the Indian population. The companies who understand these challenges and tune their strategies accordingly will surely be the winners in the years to come, taking advantage of this economic boom in the rural sector of India.

Yin & Sara (2008) in her research paper How social media and PR Connect, writes that with the emergence of social media, the whole communications landscape has transformed and the mass mobilizing power of social media is tremendous. People think that social media is a threat to traditional PR and mainstream media, however social media complements traditional PR and traditional PR will exist as an important component of any successful business. The PR and advertising agencies are all undergoing a change and are trying to evolve their strategy, physical structure and business models to be in tune with social media.

Dunne, Lawlor & Rowley (2010) in their study Young people's use of online social networking sites-a uses and gratifications perspective have made an attempt to find out the reason behind young people's use of social networking site with special reference to bebo. The results of the study indicate that the participants were using bebo for their personal motives and in order to maintain a certain persona and identity in social context. The impersonal nature of the social media has led to facilitate the young people where they can negotiate the practicalities and forge the identities and maintain relationships.

Edosomwan et al., (2011) studied the history of social media and its impacts on business. They have discussed that social media has impacted the aspects of human communication and interaction. They have examined the history of social media. They have concluded that for businesses social media sites create a kind of buzz about the brand. They have also concluded that social media is in trend because of its cost effectiveness.

Bolotaeva & Cata (2011) discussed about marketing opportunities with social networks. They have discussed about social networking sites on which users communicate, interact, share ideas and rate or give feedbacks about products and services. In this study they have discussed the advantages and risks associated with social networking sites as well as different opportunities associated with these. They have concluded that social networking sites are the best platforms for every individual as well as for business organisations to enhance their brand value.

Brown & Vaughn (2011) discussed about the use of social networking sites in hiring decisions with special reference of Facebook. They have discussed that according to different media reports, business organisations are hiring professionals through social networking sites. They have also discussed the risks associated with these sites. They have concluded that social networking sites are creating the advantages for business organisations and management should make policies regarding the risks associated with these.

Davison, Maraist & Bing (2011) studied about promises and pitfalls of using social networking sites for HR decisions. They have mentioned that different HR practices are getting influenced by the use of Internet. They have discussed about different questions associated with the use of social networking sites for the purpose of recruitment and selection. They have concluded that many HR professionals and managers are making use of the social networking sites like Facebook and LinkedIn for the purpose of recruitment, selection. In fact, there are some issues also associated with these sites which need to be resolved.

Eid and El-Gohari (2011) studied the impact of using E-Marketing on the success of marketing of small business enterprises. This study is helpful for different policy makers, practitioners, entrepreneurs, educators and researchers. This study is only focused on small business enterprises. The literature sums up that there is a quite difference between digital marketing process of small business enterprises and the large business enterprises. It is found that the most popular tools used by business enterprises for e-marketing were e-mail marketing, mobile marketing etc. It is also found that e-marketing is not only depends upon single tool but the multiple tools. They have concluded that after the survey it is found that maximum of the business organisations allocates the special budget for the marketing.

Assaad & Gomez (2011) discussed about social networks in social media marketing with different opportunities and scope. They have discussed that social networking sites are providing a very effective platform to communicate and interact globally for every individual as well as the organizations. They have concluded that companies are getting benefits from social networking sites. They have suggested that business organisations should not avoid the usage of social networking sites as these are the need of hours.

Awolusi (2012) studied the impacts of social networking sites on the workplace productivity. In this research it is studied that there is an influence of social networking sites on organisational functions like training, recruiting, communication and brand management etc. In this study it is concluded that social networking sites can influence the productivity of the workplace tremendously in terms of geographic collaboration, communication and effective marketing & promotions of products/services.

Hanafizadeh, et al (2012) studied the business impacts of social networking sites. They have discussed that social networking site like Facebook, twitter, YouTube have attracted the millions of people. These are becoming the important part for the business organizations. Business organisations are looking forward to use these sites. The results or the reviews of past literatures are suggesting that social networking sites have impacted the business organizations to a great extent.

Bhatt & Bhatt (2012) in their research paper Factors influencing Online Shopping: An Empirical Study in Ahmedabad writes about the factors which influence the perceptions of consumers regarding online shopping. The study has revealed ease/attractiveness of website, service quality of websites and website security as the three important factors which have prominently emerged from the study. The paper has proved that that these factors are related to specific type of consumers classified as occasional, frequent and regular consumers. The study shows that the regular buyers are most influenced by the ease/attractiveness and service quality of website, whereas the occasional buyers value website security to a greater extent.

Chugh (2012) threw a light on social networking a boon or bane for business organizations. He has discussed about pros as well as cons of social networking for business organizations. He has discussed that social networking sites are noble way to increase a business worldwide. He also threw light on importance of internet. He discussed that internet is promoting the social interaction globally. He has concluded that social networking sites have revolutionised the whole things in business world. They have also concluded that there is huge scope of these in future as internet is itself a future.

Constantinides, Lorenzo & Alarcón-del-Amo (2013) threw a light on social networking sites as business tool. They have discussed that social networking sites and web applications have helped the users to create the personal as well as professional relations worldwide. They have concluded that business organizations are highly interested in social networking sites as they are increasing relations as well as helping in making the different marketing and promotional strategies. They have concluded that social networking sites are effective tool for business organizations to grow.

Smits & Mogos (2013) studied the impact of social media on business performances. They have discussed that social media or social networking sites are gaining popularity and getting used in different operations of business organisations. These are becoming the essential tool for the marketing and promotional operations and functions of business organisations. They have concluded that social networking sites have enhanced the capabilities and scope for business organizations.

Stone & Woodcock (2013) explored role of latest technologies towards digital marketing making it more interactive and responsive to handle customers. They explained how business intelligence and customer insight is helping organizations in the interactive or digital marketing. They concluded that advanced support of Business Intelligence is helping the companies in the execution of processes of interactive or digital marketing. To make this process more advance and popular companies are now focusing on business intelligence and customer insight. They have further concluded that automation is playing a very important role.

Khan & Siddiqui (2013) analysed the importance of digital marketing through the exploratory study in Pakistan. They analysed digital marketing parameters and features to get a clear picture about the impacts and effectiveness of digital marketing. They concluded that latest tools of digital marketing are taking over the traditional methods of the digital marketing but still it's a new concept in Pakistan and people are getting familiar to this.

Rahadi & Abdillah (2013) studied the utilization of social networking as promotion media. They have discussed that social media or social networking sites like Facebook, twitter etc, are not acting as communication channels only but they are also acting as a promotional tool for the business. The purpose of the research is to determine a kind of model of social networking utilization as a promotional media. They have concluded that businesses are using social networking sites as promotional tools and they are getting benefits from this. Businesses are using social networking sites such as Facebook; twitter etc, because of their minimal cost, easy recognizable, global distribution areas etc.

Bhagwat & Goutam (2013) studied the concept of development of social networking sites and their different roles in business. They have taken the reference of social networking site, Facebook. They have discussed that as this world is too large to make the physical interaction. This is impossible to communicate in this huge world physically, so social networking sites are making this task easier. They have concluded that social technology connecting people and facilitating businesses in beneficial ways.

Ambrose & Catherine (2013) in their study the social media and Entrepreneurship Growth focused on the effect of social media on the growth of SMEs in Nairobi. The study established that social media tools offer greater market accessibility and CRM which in turn have a significant impact on the growth of SMEs. This study recommends that the policy makers should come up with favourable internet surfing rates and e-business policies to encourage the technological adoption that would grow the SME industry.

Thapar & Sharma (2013) in their study on role of social networking sites in some key cases throws a light on the growing popularity of social networking sites. The study showed that people have got their own media to raise their voice and stand for their rights. Author thinks that social media possess the character of true democratization of information. Study concludes that the participatory nature of Social Networking Sites cuts through caste and class barriers.

Hajli (2014) studied the impact of social media on consumers. He has discussed that social media has provided new opportunities to consumers to interact and communicate worldwide. Online communities are playing an important role in the growth and development of businesses also. He has concluded that recent advancements and technological innovations on internet have facilitated the consumers as well as the businesses.

Semeradova & Weinlich (2014) threw light on new trends in digital marketing and possibilities of their applications in marketing strategies. They have discussed the possibilities of using mobile devices in the implementation of marketing strategies for businesses. They have also discussed about creating digital marketing strategies for business houses. They have concluded business organizations can't ignore the new possibilities and trends in digital marketing.

Kumar et al. (2014) studied the factors which influence consumer buying behaviour in cosmetic products. The objective of the study is to find out internal as well as the external factors which influences the purchasing behaviour of consumers in cosmetic products. They have test different hypothesis for the study. They have found that there is the influence of different factors like cultural dimensions, aspiration groups. They have also found that there is a kind of significant difference between level of income and the social dimension of the respondents. The results also show that there is also an influence of social factors on dependents. Young people are influenced by the reference or aspiration groups.

Sathya (2015) studied the digital marketing and impact of Digital Marketing on consumer purchase. In this study it is explained that digital marketing is the medium of electronic communication among consumers and the marketers. The study is conducted on 100 consumers to clarify the different objectives like usefulness of digital marketing in the competitive market and the impact of digital marketing on the consumer purchase. It is found in the study that digital marketing has a great future and maximum consumers like it and love to purchase things online, people are aware of the terminologies of digital marketing. They concluded that digital marketing is emerging as one of the important and crucial approaches for the business organizations.

Sridevi & Kumar (2015) conducted research on emerging trends in online marketing. They have discussed about that how PC penetration has increased use of new digital tools to enhance the customer services and the product development. They have also tried to explain the different advantages of online marketing like convenience, interactive and immediate etc. They have also discussed about different types of online marketing like: online advertising, search engine marketing, email marketing etc. They have also discussed the important points like development of online marketing strategies, success of online marketing, online networking etc. They have concluded that in digital market place a good content and its presentation is considered as the most important factor which decide the fate of online marketing.

Durai & King (2015) discussed the impact of digital marketing on the growth of consumerism. They have explained that how consumerism is playing a vital role in the digitalised world. They have shared that business organisations are giving importance to digital marketing strategies and adopting digital marketing trends. They have tried to identify the factors that influence consumers with the growth of digital marketing. They have found few main factors like: consumer expectation factors, functionality factors, marketing factors and service factors. They have concluded that with the rise of internet users in India, there is a great scope of digital marketing in India. They further mentioned that business organizations need to understand the environment in which their consumers live, how they think, and how they are changing with the constant change in technology.

Parkash & Banerjee (2016) threw light on B2B business development through different channels of digital marketing. The study was focused on the Lorent Services which is one of the main services. The data was collected from the 38 companies through a well framed questionnaire which was focused on important factors like companies' comfort level towards digital marketing, reliable media, different marketing tools etc. They found that digital world is the domain with number of opportunities for the businesses to target the largest segment of the consumers. Also found that digital marketing opens different doors of opportunities for the vendors or different business houses.

Kaushik (2016) explained the concept of digital marketing in Indian context. He analysed growth of digital marketing in India. The study focuses on the different kinds of precautions must be taken for the implementation of strategies for e-marketing to get better results. He discussed trends of digital marketing through some facts and figures. He concluded that digital marketing has a great potential to raise the sale of any business and it is growing tremendously in India. As well as it is a good way to reduce the cost and increase the brand loyalty etc.

Girchenka & Ovsiannikova (2016) threw a light on digital marketing and its role in the modern business processes. They explained about different features of digital marketing along with its advantages and the disadvantages. They talked about different trends in digital marketing and compared with traditional ones. They concluded that digital marketing uses different sorts of mediums or channels to promote a product and service. Further digital marketing process is complex to execute the things as per the plan.

Wiranatha & Suryawardani (2016) explained about promoting events and festivals through digital marketing. They explained that information and communication technology is the best way to collect, analyse and disseminate the information. It is very much helpful in the decision-making process. Digital technology is moving very fast and growing rapidly for the development of the business worldwide. They recommended that advertisements play an important and crucial role in the promotional activities as well as digital advertisements create a great impact on the behaviour of the customers.

Singh (2016) discussed about impact of digital marketing on Indian rural banking. She explained that recent developments in Indian banking systems are making the operational work smooth and effective. To change the attitude of their customers, banks are taking new initiatives. She has observed that there is not a significant impact of digital marketing on rural banking. Banks are taking initiatives to automate the operations but rural customers are unable to utilize them effectively. She concluded that the customers' perception is the main thing in this regard.

Seol et al., (2016) have studied the continuance usage of social networking sites pages. This study has developed a research model that explained the continuance of social networking sites pages in business. The result suggested that quality of social interaction is one of the salient features. Audience like quality content on these pages the most. They have also discussed that these pages are getting maximum of traffic on official business websites.

Grizane & Jurgelane (2016) threw light on impacts of social media or social network on the business evaluation. The study was focused on the restaurants located in Jelgava town. They have concluded that social networking activities have changed the whole scenario of the business and impacted the ROI positively and the business gained the maximum benefits.

Can & Kaya (2016) studied the social networking sites addiction and the effect of attitude towards social network advertising. They have discussed that because of penetration of mobile devices social networking sites are becoming the world-wide phenomenon and social networking sites are giving lots of opportunities for businesses. The results of study concluded that social networking sites have partial impacts on approaches of people who are totally bonded and influenced by the advertisements on these platforms.

Banerjee (2016) presented an overview on modern trends and practices of E-Marketing. He has discussed about how internet is playing a paramount role in each and every aspect of life. He explained that marketing process have become easier with the use of internet and different digital medias. He also tried to compare eMarketing with traditional marketing by throwing light on concept and origin of e-marketing. Further he tried to explain the 7C's of eMarketing and strategies along with different advantages as well as limitations. He mentioned that future of eMarketing is promising and providing different opportunities for business organisations. He concluded that with better understanding of potential of eMarketing with giving consideration to its both advantages and limitations, business organisations can grow and face every challenge in future.

Oke et al. (2016) conducted research on behaviour of consumers towards making a decision and loyalty to particular brands. The purpose of study is to explore the different factors and determinants of consumer behaviour which can be helpful in making a decision and showing loyalty towards green tea. The study discovered different factors like convenience to buy, flavours, taste, packaging and price which influence consumers to buy the Oishi green tea. They found these factors the most influencing factors. Perception value and perceived quality have the great effect on consumer behaviour.

Pawar & Naranje (2016) conducted research on the factors which influence the buying behaviour of the customers. They have discussed that consumers are considered as the king of market and it is important to understand the need and demand of consumers. They have mentioned that consumer buying behaviour is considered as the integral and important of market strategic planning. They have focused on automobile customers and their buying behaviour in Pune city of India. They have studied the factors which influence the buying behaviour of four-wheeler car owners as well as media impact on buying behaviour factors.

After detailed research study they have concluded that in automobile industry there is a tough competition and conditions of competition are fluctuating continuously and those companies which strategize as per the change will succeed the most.

Sur (2017) studied the implications of consumer behavioural factors on customer relationship management. She has mentioned that consumer buying behaviour is the threshold of customer relationship management (CRM). She has concluded that if the organisation proved reliable to the consumers, there will be a great bond between consumer and organisation and that can lead to effective and healthy customer relationship management. The result of the study revealed that if there is only responsiveness and not any outcome, that will lead to nothing.

Lal & Singh (2017) discussed about future of business i.e. digital marketing in their descriptive study. They explained that digital marketing is the way to interact with target audience in a very less time. This review-based study focuses on the scope and potentials of digital marketing and its different paradigms. There are different findings of study like no. of internet users will be 650 million in India by 2020, mobile penetration in India etc. They have concluded that e-marketing is very much needed and essential tool or feature of a business organization and it helps to grow the business at a great pace and changing the day-by-day scenario of the business in India.

Sindhuri et al., (2017) explained about digital marketing strategies, the benefits of the digital marketing and impacts of digital marketing. They observed that digital marketing is providing the great exposure to the business worldwide, digital marketing is helping in consumer satisfaction and the impact of digital marketing on business is high enough. They concluded that digital marketing is is effective and helpful in building and maintaining the relationship with customers via different kinds of online activities. Further digital marketing is cost effective, convenient and a measurable process. Sanap (2017) studied about digital marketing in banks. She discussed about the importance and benefits of digital technologies in context of banking. She also explained about the different forms of digital marketing along with their features as well as adopted for marketing and challenges in banks. She concluded that there is growth in online banking with penetration rate of 80% adults using online banking, social media is playing an important role in this regard.

Rathore, Pant & Sharma (2017) discussed about emerging trends in digital marketing in India. They observed that Indian market is becoming technology adaptive with increasing usage. Mobile phones are dominating other human activities. Internet is in the mainstream and digital marketing is becoming the main part of the digital economy. They discussed about effective ways of digital marketing i.e. plan, manage and optimize. They also discussed about the major factors which are affecting digital marketing like literacy rate, cost, lack of knowledge and technology etc. They concluded that digital marketing is cost effective and important tool for the growth of business.

Suginraj (2017) studied about massive growth of online marketing in India. He discussed about changing scenario of Indian market. People are spending hours on Internet daily and exploring the things. Ecommerce websites are playing an important and significant role in this. He concluded that digitalization is taking place with a high speed in India and changing the whole business scenario. Different electronic gadgets are playing an important role in this growth.

Himaja (2017) discussed the social media impact on the business. In this it is discussed that web based social networking is changing the way people behave, team up, act and make things. In this study a wide research plan is plotted to make a connection between web based social networking, business and society. The study discussed that web based social networking is a new buzz word for businesses to promote the things. It is concluded that people are dependent on these technological innovations and that is creating a huge impact on businesses.

Toor, Husnain & Hussain (2017) threw light on impact of social network marketing on consumer purchase intention. They have discussed that new trends and modes of digital technologies are encroaching the traditional ones. They have also discussed that if the businesses will not shift to these changes, this may impact the outcomes of businesses drastically. They have concluded that social networking marketing influence the consumers' purchasing intentions to some extent and that is impacting the businesses.

Singh & Sinha (2017) discussed the impact of social media on performance and growth of business in India. They have discussed that social networking sites are like just another medium of communication and interaction but a large extent and scope, they cover wide areas and different innovative techniques. They have mentioned that internationally social networking sites are acting as important and essential tool for the marketing campaigns of the business organisations. They have concluded that social networking sites are impacting businesses to a great extent. These are helping business organizations in creating a great brand image.

Yadav (2017) discussed social media as a marketing tool. He has studied the opportunities and challenges in this context. He has discussed about the escalating usage of social networking sites in business world. The study is aimed to discuss how social media has affected the business performances. The paper has concluded the different benefits, scope and problems associated with use of social networking sites in business organizations.

Kannan & Li (2017) described a framework for research in the field of the digital marketing. They explained marketing strategy process with significant role and impact of digital marketing. They outlined different evolving issues in this regard like concerns for customers, environment and organizations etc. They have explained about different tools and forms of digital marketing and their benefits towards different perspectives like business growth, customer awareness and responsiveness etc.

Panganiban & Villareal (2017) threw light on strategic and tactical use of e-marketing strategies in the context of apparel industry. They explained that digital marketing is a supplementary thing for a website. Organizations use this process to create and promote their products and services. They concluded that strategic and tactical use of e-marketing strategies is effective which perceived their study on managers and employees. They have also recommended that there should be more penetration of the e-marketing strategies in different business segments to increase sales.

Akhunjonov & Obrenovic (2017) conducted research on impact of social media on consumer buying intention. They have mentioned that earlier business organisations were using print media, television etc. for advertising purposes, but now they are seeking for new ways of marketing and advertising. The purpose of the study to find out how social media and brand perception can help to find different emerging opportunities to increase the engagement with customers. They have reviewed the past literature for this. They have concluded that with the increase in social media channels worldwide, business and customers engagement has increased. Business organisations are integrating different strategies for targeting and engaging with customers.

Alnsour (2018) conducted quantitative research on the different effects of social media on purchase intention of the consumers with the research focus on Jordanian Airlines Industry. He discussed that how different social media benefits affect the purchase intention of the customers of airline industry. He used exploratory method to conduct the further research and defined different research hypothesis. He calculated the data through well designed questionnaire and used different statistical tools to analyse data. He has concluded that there is the positive effect of monetary and hedonic benefits of social media on consumers' purchase intention and there is no relationship between purchase intention and functional and social benefits of social media.

Akar & Dalgic (2018) conducted research on online consumers and their purchase intentions. This have used the social network theory and theory of planned behaviour to analyse the behaviour of online consumers. They have target twitter users to conduct the research analysis because of few factors like: popularity of twitter, market penetration, popularity, and open-source data. This study will guide the business organizations and e-marketers to create and design the marketing strategies for their business.

Victor et al. (2018) studied factors which influences consumer behaviour and the purchase decisions in price dynamic environment. They have followed the exploratory factor analysis approach. They have discussed about the new technological advancements. They have conducted the primary research survey of 178 samples. They have analysed the seven factors to determine the consumer behaviour. In this study it is concluded that there is need to understand the consumer behaviour with respect to dynamic pricing.

Gibson (2018) explained about the different strategies and approaches used in digital marketing to promote a business. He has explained that businesses are implementing digital marketing strategies and approaches as their primary strategies to promote a product or service. He concluded that there are different type of digital marketing strategies and approaches, quite useful for the successful running of a business.

Henderson (2018) studied the role of social media or social networking sites in recruitment and selection process. He has discussed that in present scenario maximum of the organizations are hiring employees by making use of social networking sites. He has concluded that there are different characteristics and concerns like professionalism etc, recruiters look for in candidate during the recruitment and selection process.

Shirisha (2018) studied the importance of the digital marketing in the new era with the analysis of secondary data. She explained the different forms of digital marketing and the different channels of the digital marketing available. She also discussed the role of internet in digital marketing and further added various benefits of digital marketing over the traditional marketing. She also highlighted the Indian perspective of online advertising. She finally concluded that digital marketing plays a vital role in the growth of the business.

Bala & Verma (2018) did a critical review of digital marketing with the help of secondary data. In this study they have acknowledged that businesses are really getting benefited by digital marketing as well as from different tools of digital marketing. They discussed current and future trends of digital marketing. They concluded that India is experiencing a radical change towards the digitalization. Consumers are spending maximum of their time on internet or social media channels. Further they concluded that the businesses are getting benefits from SEO, SEM, SMM, email marketing, influencer marketing etc. They also concluded that the whole process of digital marketing is cost effective and have great impact on the businesses because of its vast reach.

Slijepcevic & Radojevic (2018) discussed about current trends in digital marketing communication. The objective of the research to discuss the communication in digital marketing and their impact on company environment. They have discussed about different tools and communication medias in digital marketing. They have concluded that development of internet and mobile internet is changing the whole business scenarios and impacting the organizations at large. With the use of these technologies' companies are improving their strategies and different modes of marketing communication.

Devraj & Renuka (2018) explained about digital marketing and different forms of digital marketing with advantages of digital marketing over traditional marketing. They concluded that business houses are getting serious about digital marketing and are doing more investments in this. Different channels of digital marketing are becoming main part of business strategy. Small to large scale enterprises have started investing in digital marketing.

Vetrivel & Balachandran (2018) explained the role of digital marketing in modern business. They explored that digital marketing is playing an important and crucial role in marketing strategies of organizations. Specialized areas of digital marketing like SEO, SEM, SMM, email marketing etc are playing different roles in digital marketing. They also discussed about importance of digital marketing with different advantages over the traditional marketing. They concluded that digital marketing process is not the overnight process, it takes time and lot of patience.

Murgai (2018) explained about transforming digital marketing with artificial intelligence. He has discussed that because of rapid development in information technology and its applications, the whole business scenario is changed throughout the world. This paper discusses about the most probable sectors in digital marketing where artificial intelligence has made its presence. He has discussed about the role of artificial intelligence in business and business transactions. He has thrown light on the relationship between digital marketing and artificial intelligence. He concluded that technological advancements always create different opportunities for business organisations throughout the world. He also added that artificial intelligence is creating a buzz in this field of digital space.

Ramya & Ali (2018) studied the consumer buying behaviour in departmental store in Coimbatore city of India. This study focuses on examination of consumer buying behaviour towards Amul products. Through a convenient sampling technique, they have taken data from 150 consumers through questionnaire. They have concluded that promotional product strategies can be improved to increase the sale. They also mentioned that as buying behaviour of the consumer is positive, there is a great future of the product in the city.

Koyluoglu et al (2018) conducted research on consumer behaviour with special reference of Konya city of Turkey. They have mentioned that understanding the consumer behaviour have become an essential competitive tool for business organisations. They highlighted that consumer behaviours are the situations that may be finished with purchasing or not. They have also discussed about the buying behaviour of consumers. They have also discussed the factors which determine the buying behaviour of the consumer. They have concluded that consumer get benefit from service, product quality, price, reliability etc.

Shah (2018) studied the impact of digital marketing on business and politics. He threw light on few facts like there are approx. 500 million and above are agile internet users in India. And on an average approx. 281 million access the internet daily. These are enough data to show the dominance of digital marketing on business as well as in politics. He has discussed that digital channels provide a great opportunity for business organisations to interact and communicate with the customers. He has concluded that it is quite obvious that digital marketing has increased the level of interaction of business organisations and politicians with Indians.

Rajaiah (2019) discussed about their research on future and growth of digital marketing in India. They have mentioned that scope and future of digital marketing in India is going to be brighter. They have also discussed about the need of mobile phones. As the number of internet users are increasing in India, there is the great opportunity for business organisations to target a vast audience to sell their products and services. They have discussed about different government initiative regarding digital operations. They have also mentioned about different forms of digital marketing. They have concluded that digital marketing is growing with the rapid pace throughout the world and digital marketing industry is booming with a great pace. They have also concluded that business organisations.

Telreja et al (2019) studied about the concept of Facebook – which is a boon or bane for social media marketing. They have discussed that Facebook is dominating the global market continuously because of its unique innovative characteristics and features. They have discussed about different opportunities provided by social networking sites for businesses. They have concluded that social networking sites or social media marketing providing a great platform of advertisement for the business organisations.

Ayswarya et al., (2019) studied about the concept of Facebook – which is a boon or bane for social media marketing. They have discussed that Facebook is dominating the global market continuously because of its unique innovative characteristics and features. They have discussed about different opportunities provided by social networking sites for businesses. They have concluded that social networking sites or social media marketing providing a great platform of advertisement for the business organisations.

Makrides et al. (2019) explained about digital marketing and its transformative impacts on the companies and business world. In this study there are different platforms and segments are analysed which helpful to increase the brand awareness internationally. It is also explained that digital marketing is contributing a lot for medium small enterprises and introduction of different digital marketing techniques (like Social Media Marketing, Email Marketing etc.) are serving different market segments.

Dash & Sharma (2019) discussed about the impact of digital marketing on the luxury car brands. This study has proposed a marketing response model for luxury car brands. The result of study has shown that digital marketing medium is providing the best responses than newspapers, magazines and display events.

Aggarwal & Verma (2019) explained the emerging trends in Digital Marketing. They have discussed about different objectives of digital marketing. They have also explained the different current and future trends in digital marketing like: influencer marketing, social messaging apps, chatbots, programming ads, YouTube ads etc. They have concluded that digital marketing is the need of hours in industry. Without the usage of digital marketing, businesses can face different strategy related drawbacks.

Srinivasulu & Rajaiah (2019) discussed about their research on future and growth of digital marketing in India. They have mentioned that scope and future of digital marketing in India is going to be brighter. They have also discussed about the need of mobile phones. As the number of internet users are increasing in India, there is the great opportunity for business organisations to target a vast audience to sell their products and services. They have discussed about different government initiative regarding digital operations. They have also mentioned about different forms of digital marketing. They have concluded that digital marketing is growing with the rapid pace throughout the world and digital marketing industry is booming with a great pace. They have also concluded that business organisations need to embrace the digital changes and adopt new technological changes.

Sharma et al. (2020) have discussed about involvement of digital marketing in travel agencies. The purpose of the study is to get an idea whether travel agencies are making use of digital marketing for their business or not? In this study it is found that some of the travel agencies are making use of traditional marketing and majority of travelling agencies are making use of both traditional as well as digital marketing tools. It is also found that social media and websites are popular among all other.

Sharma (2020) studied the impact of social media marketing on consumer buying behaviour. She has conducted research on 220 respondents through a questionnaire. She has discussed that online networking advertising is creating a huge opportunity for the business organisations. She mentioned that advertisers need to understand the web-based life is affecting the purchaser's purchasing conduct. She has concluded that there is a direct positive relation between consumer buying decision making and social media marketing. She also concluded that we can anticipate consumer buying decision making with social media marketing.

Research Gap

A research gap is a problem, issue or we can say, a question which is not answered in the past studies within a particular field. Research gap can be of different types which is explained in the following figure:

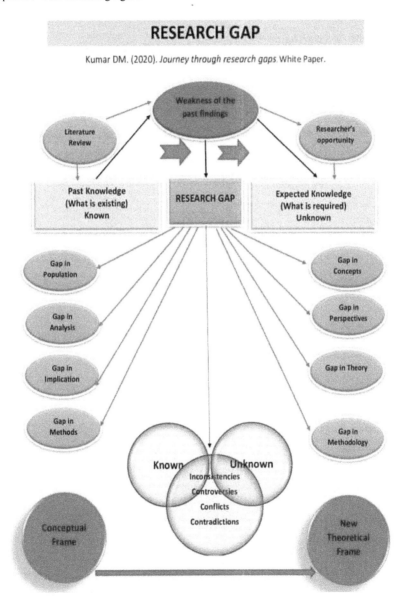

Figure: 2.1 Types of Research Gap

59

After the comprehensive literature review which is discussed above in this chapter, there are few research gaps which are identified.

- Review of literature have revealed that there are very less attempts made to study the different impacts of digital marketing on business organisations in Indian context.
- There is a lack of studies in which the different motivational factors for adoption of digital marketing have been studied.
- Very few studies have been studied the different modes of digital marketing which are effective for the business organisation in their overall growth.
- Maximum of the studies available related to digital marketing haven't vastly studied the different challenges faced by the business organisations during the adoption of digital marketing.
- Very few studies have been discussed the role of digital marketing and social media channels in context of customers.

These are some of the research or literature gaps, which are identified after the review of literature. Keeping in view the above discussed considerations, there is a requirement or need to conduct research or undertake a study which can study the impact of digital marketing on business organisations in Indian context. From the literature, it is cleared that the marketing concept is getting modernisation as the internet and technological influence and dominance is increasing with time. As India has started following the different schemes of Government like "Start-up India", "Make in India", "Stand-up India" and "Digital India", individuals are thinking of starting their own ventures, start-ups. In this, Digital Marketing can be a very much effective, efficient and helpful aspect for the growth of their start-up or business. These things generate a curiosity to study the different impacts of digital marketing with their motivational factors as well as the challenges in the adoption so that it can be easy for the business organisation to make strategies accordingly. The current study can be one of the important steps that can be needed to bridge the identified gaps and efforts made so far in the past studies.

In this chapter, an effort is made to study the past studies and identify the available research gaps. This is useful to clarify the concept and make an understanding about the present study. In the next chapter the Research Methodology is discussed in which different components included like the need, scope of the study, research design, statistical methods, development of research instrument, objectives, hypothesis and limitations etc.

The current study focuses on the impacts of digital marketing on Indian business organisations as well as customers' perceptions towards digital marketing and advertising. To attain the study's stated goals and objectives, a systematic and scientific technique is used. This chapter, titled Research Methodology, covers a wide range of topics, including the study's need, research issues, scope, research design, and projected outcomes. The following are some of the components of a study design: sample, sampling methodologies, research instruments, data gathering methods, data analysis tools and techniques, and so on.

3.1 Definition of Problem

One of the most important and crucial aspects of the research process is defining the research problem. A research problem is essentially a statement about a concerned area; it could be a scenario or condition that needs to be improved, a query or problem that can be answered or eliminated in previous studies, literature, or alternative theories. To obtain good research results, it is critical to adequately identify a research problem by taking into account several characteristics or factors. Poorly specified research problems can cause a slew of issues, misunderstandings, and problems, all of which can have a detrimental impact on research design and study or research findings.

Following the evaluation or in-depth examination of previous studies, existing literature, and discussions with many research professionals, the research problem for present study is defined as:

"A Study on the Impact of Digital Marketing on Indian Firms"

3.2 Need and Importance of Study

As technical improvements and advancements are growing at a pace in all the sectors, Digital Marketing has become an important and vital feature or factor for business organisations in all sectors. Market research is one of the most important considerations for any firm looking to gain a significant competitive advantage in the marketplace. The current study, titled "A Study on the Impact of Digital Marketing on Indian Enterprises," focuses on understanding the many types of impacts of digital marketing on Indian firms, as well as customer perceptions of digital marketing or one of its subsets, digital advertising. Firms will have a detailed understanding of the various functions of digital marketing, its good and negative effects, as well as what customers think about this growing technical breakthrough in the field of marketing, i.e., digital marketing, by following the findings of this study. The opinions and impressions of customers are critical to every company's success. This work is significant since there is relatively little research being done on this topic, and there are very few specific papers available in this sector. The study's conclusions and findings will aid businesses that are utilising or planning to use digital marketing in the future in understanding the role, scope, and impact of digital marketing on businesses.

3.3 Scope of Study

Scope of digital marketing is tremendously increasing. As internet is continuously dominating the world. It has changed the lifestyle of every individual as people are spending maximum of their time on internet or working over internet. The current study has wide scope for business organisations in different sectors as study has been carried out to find out different impacts of digital marketing on Indian firms and also the perception of customers about digital marketing. This will help to solve different future research issues and helps the business organisations as well as the customers in decision making. This study will bring out the different factors of digital marketing which are impacting the businesses positively or negatively so that businesses will get to know whether to make use of digital marketing or not. This study will also reveal challenges faced by businesses in implementation of digital marketing strategies. The results and findings of the study will help the businesses which are using or starting digital marketing to know the role, scope and impact of digital marketing on businesses in future.

3.4 Research Issues

The Internet is increasingly dominating the world in different ways. In the present scenario, everyone has easy access to internet. People are spending a maximum of their time on internet by using media like smartphones, laptops, and other electronic gadgets. This lifestyle has attracted business organizations to shift their marketing approach towards digital marketing. They are making use of digital technologies to expand their penetration vis a vis market share. By keeping the implications of digital marketing into consideration and research gaps in the relevant field, the following research issues are proposed in the present research. What are the different worldwide trends in the usage of digital marketing? Which of digital marketing tools and techniques (SEO, SEM, SMM, Email Marketing, Content Marketing, etc.) is helping the business organizations to grow more?

- What are the favorable factors towards adoption of digital marketing? How government and other forces playing a significant role in the adoption of digital marketing?

- What is the cost of campaign setup, infrastructure, and other basic requirements and facilities?

- What benefits business organizations are getting after the adoption of digital marketing? Which factors encourage business organizations most towards the adoption of digital marketing? What strategies are being used by business organizations to reap the maximum benefits of digital marketing?

- What are the challenges and benefits business organizations are facing after the adoption of the same? How digital marketing is impacting their sales, marketing share, customer relationship management, etc?

- What are the perceptions of consumers toward digital marketing? How do they perceive digital marketing? Are they influenced by digital marketing or not? Which form of digital marketing appeals most to them?

- How social media presence is important for business organizations? Businesses are getting benefits from their presence on social media channels or not. Which social media channel is more effective for business organizations like (Facebook, Twitter, Instagram, Tumblr, Whatsapp etc.)

- What will be the impact of upcoming technologies like 5G, artificial intelligence, machine learning etc. on digital marketing adoption?

Digital marketing is becoming the increasing need of hour as it is impacting businesses and consumers in several ways. On the basis of above research issues, the research objectives for the present study are framed as, To study the emergence of digital marketing in the Indian scenario (YOY secondary data analysis); To identify the factors that motivates adoption of digital marketing; To identify the challenges or problems faced by the firms during adoption or implementation; To measure the impact of digital marketing on the sales of business firms; To identify the most effective mode of digital marketing that influences firms; To identify the most effective social media channel that influences business organisations to adopt digital marketing and To analyse customers' perception towards digital marketing. In order to meet theses research objectives following hypothesis formulated for this research work.

3.5 Hypothesis

H_1^1: Identified motivating factors are influencing in adoption of digital marketing for business firms.

H_1^2: There is a significance difference between the challenges faced by the firms and motivational factors in the adoption of digital marketing.

H_1^3: There is an impact of digital marketing modes on business growth.

H_1^4: There are effective modes of digital marketing channels that influence firms to adopt digital marketing.

H_1^5: Digital marketing does influence consumers decision making.

H_1^6: Social Media Channels are the most influential and essential subsets of Digital Marketing.

3.6 Research Methodology

In the previous chapter, Review of literature is discussed. That is helpful in finding the gap between present studies, which contribute to plan research methodology to achieve the set objectives. Research Methodology is the systematic or a well-planned way of solving a research problem. It is the combination of different sampling techniques, data collection methods, the time to complete the study, the number of respondents, and different tools used for the analysis. In simple words, research methodology is the set of different methods used to conduct successful research. This chapter explains the scope of study, need of study, and the research design followed. The research design contains the different arrangements of several components like sample, research instruments, method of data collection and analysis tools etc. For the present study, primary as well as secondary data shall be used. For the collection of primary data, I will select different companies (respondents) who are making use of digital marketing tools and techniques from the last two years and more.

For this purpose, convenient random sampling technique will be used and the data will be collected through well-designed questionnaires. The questionnaire will be divided into three parts i.e., first part will contain questions based on demographic profile of the respondents, second part will contain questions based on how digital marketing is impacting the businesses and the third part will contain the questions to check the perception of consumers toward digital marketing or advertising. To analyse the collected data various statistical test, tools will be used as per requirement of the study. The sources of secondary data will be a newspaper, magazines, online portals, official websites, articles, research papers, journals, annual reports, and various textbooks.

3.6.1 Research Design

Research design is basically a framework or an arrangement of different techniques and research methods. Research design is basically a design or structure before the commencement of complete research process. Research design basically deals with logical problem, not with logistical problem (Yin, 1989: 29). Generally, research design consists a well-defined research problem or statement, different tools and techniques used, sample to be studied, methods which are going to be used in analysis of collected data. There are generally three main types of a research design which are described as follow:

3.6.1.1 Exploratory Research Design

Exploratory research basically emphases on the discovery of new insights and ideas. This is the research which is used to investigate a kind of problem which is not perfectly or clearly defined. This study does not provide a conclusive result. Exploratory research is generally carried out when the research problem or issue is at preliminary or introductory stage. It helps in tackling the new problems on which there are no previous research or very few researches have been done. It generally focuses on secondary data to study. Usually, it is said that exploratory research is employed when the research problem is new or at initial stage and data is difficult to collect. It is very much flexible and adaptive to change.

3.6.1.2 Descriptive Research Design

Descriptive research is a type of research which is concerned in describing a particular group an individual, a situation or a phenomenon. It generally answers the questions which are in what, how, when, where form. This is the type of research which explores research issues or problems in a very deep manner beyond the surface level and provide detailed description about the research subject. One of the uniqueness of descriptive research is that it can explore both the qualitative as well as the quantitative research methods. Descriptive research can be helpful in solving real life problems related to various fields. Descriptive research generally uses three type of data collection methods which are:

- Observational method
- Case study method
- Survey research method (Online as well as offline survey)

3.6.1.3 Experimental Research Design

Experimental research design is considered as one of the most known research designs for fields like physical sciences and other related fields. This type of research designs focuses more on reduction of biasness and increase in reliability. These type of research designs are considered as the standard research design. These are suitable to examine the cause effect relationship in research problem.

3.6.2 Sampling

The present research: **"A Study on the Impacts of Digital Marketing on Indian Firms"** is accentuating more to study different impacts of digital marketing on Indian firms of different sectors and also the perception of customers about digital marketing or advertising. The study is divided into two parts. The first part is associated to carry the research on Indian firms to study different motivational factors towards the use of digital marketing, the challenges and issues firms are facing after the use of digital marketing.

Table 3.1: Industrial Sample Description

1.	Population/Sample	The firms using digital marketing or different modes of digital marketing for the purpose of promotion and advertisements of their product and services. (Region: North India)
2.	Sampling Frame	List of the firms
3.	Sampling Method	a) Random Sampling Method for the identification of Firms b) Convenience Sampling Method for the collection of data
4.	Sample Size	Selected 500 and finalized 420 after data cleaning and scrutiny.

Source: Framed Structure

Data of 420 participants were collected from four business types i.e., proprietorship firm, partnership firm, Corporation and semi-government based on convenient sampling method. There are few participants of other kinds of business as well. Industries like healthcare, IT sector, education, production and manufacturing, food and hospitality, tour and travels and banking sector etc., had been contacted for data collection. The second part of the study is to check the perception of consumers towards digital marketing.

Table 3.2: Customers' Sample Description

1	Population/Sample	Customers are selected from different socio-economic and demographic backgrounds who are the internet users and have knowledge about digital marketing and advertisements.
2	Sampling Frame	List of the customers
3	Sampling Method	Random and Convenience Sampling Method
4	Sample Size	Selected 600 customers and finalized 563 after data cleaning and scrutiny.

Source: Framed Structure

For this, data of 600 online customers have been collected via Google form and one to one interaction on the basis of different socio-economic or demographic backgrounds. After data cleaning and scrutiny process, 563 customers have been finalized for further analysis. The selected 563 customers were internet users and have a knowledge of digital marketing or online advertisements.

3.6.3 Data Collection

The current study was based on both primary as well as secondary data. Secondary data was collected through existing literature of digital marketing, different subsets of digital marketing and consumer behaviour, annual reports of the organisations, magazines, reputed journals, official websites and different verified data providing portals etc. Primary data of study was collected with the help of well-designed questionnaire. Questionnaire was designed by keeping all the necessary factors and all concerned objectives in mind. The questionnaire was divided into two parts. The first part was to get the data from Indian firms and second part was to check the perception of customers towards digital marketing or advertising. Maximum of the statements were measured on Likert's Five Point Scale, few questions were in the form of Yes/No. Some questions were also on rating and ranking.

3.7 Statistical Tool and Techniques

The data collected from different sources the results are mentioned in the tabular form as per the requirement of the analysis. For this purpose, different tools and techniques are used, which are explained in the following section.

A) Mathematical Tools: In the present study, different mathematical tools like percentage have been used in the analysis of collected data.

i) Tabular Analysis

Tabular analysis is a scientific analysis. In this type of analysis, the percentage values are calculated to find out the results. In the current study, the tabular analysis is used to draw some of the main results.

ii) Ranking Analysis

Ranking method of analysis is used to check the different aspects like, very important factor, the most effective factor or aspect, preferences, favourability etc. In the current study, ranking analysis method was used to find out the most effective and preferred social media channel for the business organisations.

B) Statistical Methods

Statistical methods provide the essential tools for collecting, organising, analysing and interpreting the collected primary as well as secondary data. The two main statistical methods used in the current study are:

- Descriptive Statistical Methods
- Hypothesis Testing Methods

a) Descriptive Statistical Methods

These are the type of methods which are generally used to describe the different characteristics of a sample of the defined population. According to Riffenburgh RH (2012), numerical summaries of different datasets is known as descriptive statistics. There are four major methods of descriptive statistics.

- Measures of frequency – Percentages, Frequency etc.
- Measures of central tendency – Mean, Median, Mode etc.
- Measures of dispersions or variations – Range, Variance, Standard Deviation etc.
- Measures of position – Percentile Ranks, Quartile ranks etc.

For the current study, the different combination of these descriptive methods is used to analyse the collected data.

Mean or Arithmetic Mean

Mean is also termed as Arithmetic Mean, which is the most common measures of central tendency. The formula to calculate Arithmetic mean is:

Arithmetic Mean, $\bar{X} = \frac{\Sigma X}{N}$

In the current study, mean values are used to find out the challenges in the adoption of the digital marketing.

Standard Deviation

To quantify the degree or amount of dispersion or variation in data values, standard deviation is one of the most effective method to be followed. It is also represented by the Greek letter sigma 'σ'. The low of value of sigma means the low deviation which further means that the data values are tend to be closed to mean value. This is worked out as:

$$\text{Standard Deviation, } \sigma = \sqrt{\frac{\Sigma(X-\bar{X})^2}{N}}$$

Skewness

Skewness is the measure of asymmetry. According to the Morris Hamburg, "Skewness refers to the lack or symmetry in the shape of a frequency distribution." Simpson and Kafka defined it as, "Measure of skewness tell us the direction and the extent of skewness. In symmetrical distribution the mean, median and mode are identical. More the mean moves away from the mode, the larger will be the asymmetry and skewness.

$$\text{Coefficient of } SK_p = \frac{\text{Mean} - \text{Mode}}{\text{Standard Deviation}}$$

From the above definitions it is cleared that when a distribution is not symmetrical, it is called skewed distribution.

Kurtosis

In Greek, Kurtosis means "bulginess". As per statistics, kurtosis means the degree of peakedness or flatness in a frequency distribution. The degree of kurtosis is measured relative to the peakedness of normal curve. The value of coefficient of kurtosis is the most important measure which is shown as β_2.

Correlation Analysis

The correlation analysis is used to identify or to find out the relationship between the independent and dependent variables. This method also shows the interdependency among the variables. Coefficient of correlation is a real number that exists between -1 to +1.

General formula for the same is: $r = \dfrac{\Sigma xy}{\sqrt{x^2.y^2}}$

Where r = Karl Pearson's Coefficient of Correlation

$x = (X - \bar{X})$

$y = (Y - \bar{Y})$

b) Hypothesis Testing Methods

ANOVA (F-Test)

ANOVA is also known as "Analysis of Variance". It is the statistical method which is used to analyse the difference between group means and their associations. In the present study, ANOVA (One-way ANOVA) has been applied to find the different level of significances in the data set. In this the F values is calculated which means if F value is greater than 0.05, then it is said to be significant value. The general formula for the calculation is:

$$F = \dfrac{\text{Explained Variance}}{\text{Unexplained Variance}}$$

Or

$$F = \dfrac{\text{Between Group Variability}}{\text{Within Group Variablity}}$$

Chi Square Test

The chi-square test is one of the simplest kinds of test which comes under the category of non-parametric test. The chi-square describes the magnitude of the discrepancy between observation and theory. The formula of calculation is:

$$\chi^2 = \Sigma \dfrac{(O = E)^2}{E}$$

Where:

O = Observed Frequencies
E = Expected Frequencies

72

E = Row Total x Column Total ÷ Grand Total

The calculated value of the chi-square is compared with the table value of the chi-square for a given degree of freedom. Chi-square value is always considered positive.

Factor Analysis

Factor analysis is a statistical technique which is multivariate in nature. This technique is used to simplify or reduce the multiple variables known as factors. In the present study, factor analysis is used to identify the motivational factors in the adoption of digital marketing. There are different measures which are associated with factor analysis, which are:

Kaiser-Meyer-Olkin (KMO)

Kaiser-Meyer-Olkin (KMO) is the measure of sampling adequacy. This catalogue is also used to determine the appropriateness of factor analysis. The values between "0.5-1" indicates that the factor analysis is appropriate. Below 0.5 the factor analysis is considered as inappropriate.

Bartlett's test of Sphericity

Bartlett's test of sphericity helps in assessing whether the correlation matrix is an identity matrix or not. The varimax rotation based on eigenvalues should be greater than 1. This test is basically an indication of relationship strength among variables.

Correlation Matrix

Correlation matrix is the matrix which shows the coefficients of correlation in tabular form. The diagonal of the correlation matrix is always set to ones. This is because the correlation between a variable and itself is always 1.

Eigen Value

The total variance explained by each factor is represented by eigen values. The sum of the eigen values can't be more than the number of items considered for the purpose of analysis.

Scree Plot

Scree plot is useful in the determination of the factors to retain in Exploratory Factor Analysis (EFA). It is the graph between eigen values and the number of factors.

3.8 Questionnaire Development

For the present study following process has been followed:

- Statement of the theoretical construct
- Construction of the questionnaire
- Pre-Testing of the questionnaire
- Purification of the questionnaire
- Finalization of the questionnaire
- Processing and validation of the questionnaire

In this study, in order to achieve research objectives, we have framed two separate questionnaires, i.e., first one was developed for business firms and second for customers. The process of questionnaire development is discussed in the following two sections (A and B).

A. Development of Questionnaire to study the Impacts of Digital Marketing on Indian Firms

3.8.1 Statement of the Theoretical Construct

Factor That Motivates Business Firms to Adopt Digital Marketing

For the purpose of scale development for research and establishment of preliminary bounce to construct a comprehensive literature review related to digital marketing impact and consumers' perception was conducted. The important components of the questionnaire are described briefly in the following paragraphs.

To begin with these objectives, different factors were identified with the help of comprehensive literature review. For this Technology Acceptance Model (TAM) (Davis, 1989) was used. This is designed to measure the new technology acceptance of individuals or groups. This model basically works on two measures which are, Perceived Usefulness which is the construct of Technology Acceptance Model (TAM). It means to what extent an individual believes that using a specific technology will enhance their knowledge as well as productivity (Davis, 1989). Perceived Ease of Use which is also one of the important independent constructs of Technology Acceptance Model (TAM). According to Davis, it means, to what extent a person believes that using a specific system would be free of effort or very less efforts (Davis, 1989, p. 320). In the objective i.e., Motivation towards the adoption of Digital Marketing, the factors are identified with the help of comprehensive literature review which somehow contribute towards the Technology Acceptance Model (TAM) too. A study (El-Gohary, Trueman and Fukukawa, 2009) focused on the factors like Organisational factors, Technological Factors, Business Environment factors (consisting internal as well as external environment), which are controllable and uncontrollable. These are the factors which are directly or indirectly contribute towards TAM also. Some other studies like (Eze *et al.*, 2020), (Ritz, Wolf and McQuitty, 2019), (Abu Bakar and Ahmed, 2015), (El-Gohary and Eid, 2012), (Abraham, 2018), have also used Changing Customers' Attitude, Organizational Factors, Technological Factors, Management Factors, Business Environment Factors etc. in their respective studies to find out the desired significant results.

Combining all these past studies, there was an agreement that, motivation towards adoption of digital marketing should be evaluated on the basis of these factors like:

- Changing Customers' Attitude
- Organizational Factors
- Technological Factors
- Management Factors
- Business Environment Factors

For all these five factors, there were 21 statements framed to evaluate the motivation towards adoption of digital marketing in firms.

Challenges Faced by The Firms During Adoption of Digital Marketing

For this objective of the study, different challenges identified after conducting comprehensive literature review and genuine published articles on web. Few studies like (El-Gohary, Trueman and Fukukawa, 2009), (Leeflang *et al.*, 2014), (Ištvanić, Milić and Krpić, 2017) etc. have identified few challenges like management of the received data, government policies, lack of finance, identification of right tools and technology, training of staff, changing customers' behaviour etc. So, after combining all these challenges identified from the past studies and the inputs received from the digital marketing experts, following challenges were framed for the study:

- Data Management
- Identification and selection of right technology
- Training of Team/Staff
- Customer's/employees' Changing behaviour and experience
- Development of digital marketing strategies
- Analysis of the competition
- Lack of finance
- Government Policies

Modes of Digital Marketing and Their Impact on Sales of Business: To study these objectives in the present study, different research articles were reviewed to chalk out some modes of digital marketing used and were found effective and also responsible for the increase in the sale of business firms. Studies like (Peter, M. K. and Dalla Vecchia, M. 2020), (Kennedy Onyango, 2016), (Eid and El-Gohary, 2013), (Sotnikova, 2016), (Kannan and Li, 2017), (El-Gohary, Trueman and Fukukawa, 2009) have identified few modes of digital marketing like Affiliate Marketing, Search Engine Marketing (SEM), Social Media Marketing (SMM), E-Mail Marketing, Pay Per Click (PPC), Content Marketing etc. which are also influencing in terms of increasing the sale of business firms. So, after analysing the past studies and discussion with few research and digital marketing experts some modes of digital marketing are identified for the present study which are mentioned below:

- Social Media Marketing (SMM)
- Search Engine Marketing (SEM)
- Affiliate Marketing

- Content Marketing
- E-Mail Marketing
- Search Engine Optimization (SEO)

3.8.2 Preliminary Draft of the Questionnaire Developed for Business Firms

A set of total 21 statements was constructed preliminary for the five identified motivating factors responsible for the adoption of digital marketing and 26 Statements was constructed for other objectives.

Table 3.3: Preliminary Draft of the Questionnaire Developed for Business Firms

Sr. No.	Factors	Statements	Total
1.	Changing Consumers Attitude	1,2,3,4	4
2.	Organizational Factors	5,6,7,8	4
3.	Technological Factors	9,10,11,12,13	5
4.	Management Factors	14,15,16,17	4
5.	Business Environment Factors	18,19,20,21	4
6.	Challenges during the adoption of Digital Marketing	1,2,3,4,5,6,7,8	8
7.	Effective Modes of Digital Marketing	1,2,3,4,5,6	6
8.	Modes of Digital Marketing Impacting Sales of Business	1,2,3,4,5	5
9.	Social Media Channels	1,2,3,4,5,6,7	7
		Total	**47**

Source: Primary Data

The table represents the preliminary draft of the first objective of the questionnaire which is to evaluate the different objectives of the study, which was pre-tested on appropriate sample (Refer Annexure 1 for Preliminary Questionnaire)

8.6.3   Pre-Testing, Purification, Validation of the Pre-Questionnaire (Firms)

Preliminary drafted first part of the questionnaire was pre-tested by doing reliability analysis on framed 21 statements of Motivating Factors and 26 statements of other objectives of the study to assess the internal consistency of the data based on Cronbach's alpha and Factor wise analysis.

Reliability Analysis

Reliability is done via SPSS on 21 statements of Motivating Factors and 26 statements of other objectives. Here data reliability is assessed to check the internal consistency of the data based on Cronbach's alpha. Here the fundamental analysis is done at 95% confidence level. According to (J.C Nunnally, 1978), (L.J Cronbach, 1951), offered a thumb rule of 0.70. An alpha value greater than 0.70 is considered to be suitable for further analysis. According to (L.J Cronbach, 1951), the table below presents Cronbach's alpha range and adequacy level.

Table 3.4: Cronbach Alpha Adequacy

S.NO	Cronbach's Alpha	Adequacy
1	0.9 & above	Excellent
2	0.8-0.89	Good
3	0.7-0.79	Fair
4	0.6-0.69	Marginal
5	0.59 & below	Poor

Source: (L.J Cronbach, 1951)

Here as per the gathered data, the overall Cronbach value is close to 0.765 for 26 statements. This infers that gathered data can be used for further analysis.

Table 3.5: Reliability Analysis

Reliability Statistics	
Cronbach's Alpha	No. of Items
0.765	26

Source: Primary Data

This also assumes that there is a fair consistency found in the collected data of 420 participants. A good consistency is found for the further analysis.

For the reliability of 21 statements of motivating factors of digital marketing, Factor wise analysis was performed by using factor analysis technique. The item statistics represents the values of the would-be Cronbach's alpha value if the particular item or statement is deleted. Here none of the statement value is less than the tolerance limit of 0.70. that is why all the statements are used in the analysis. Regarding item correlation, the lowest value is close to - 1.4%, with an alpha value of 0.762%.

Hence this statement is not removed from further analysis. The average mean and standard deviation of the data is close to 3.68±1.25. Not much deviation from the mean has been observed in the identified data.

Table 3.6: Reliability Analysis of factors motivating for the adoption of digital marketing

Statements	Mean	Std. Deviation	Item Correlation	Cronbach's Alpha
Customers are spending sufficient time over the internet because it is easy to access.	3.64	1.440	0.146	0.752
Customers find it convenient to interact through Digital Marketing.	3.64	1.440	0.393	0.731
Consumers' preference has changed from traditional media (TV, radio, newspaper, etc.) to digital media (blogs, social media, website, apps, etc.)	3.81	1.381	0.499	0.722
More customized messages can be communicated through digital marketing.	3.70	1.372	0.475	0.724
The availability of financial resources makes it possible for the organization to adopt digital marketing.	3.63	1.046	0.538	0.724
Advanced technological infrastructure in an organization encourages to the adoption of digital marketing.	3.89	1.016	0.539	0.724
Digital Marketing is becoming a part of the workstyle due to the continued dominance of the internet and technology.	3.78	1.116	0.468	0.727
With the use of digital marketing tools, the productivity of the organization has	3.92	1.053	0.582	0.721

increased.				
Technological advancements make it convenient to adopt digital marketing.	3.72	1.234	0.517	0.722
Deployment of Artificial Intelligence (AI), chatbots, etc. personalized digital marketing campaigns	3.56	1.317	0.360	0.734
Technological innovations in digital marketing are helpful to increase the effectiveness of promotional and marketing activities on a digital platform.	3.42	1.389	0.312	0.738
The adoption of modern technologies reduces the cost of marketing on a digital platform.	3.66	1.316	0.470	0.725
Data management is not a challenge in the adoption of digital marketing.	3.64	1.145	0.312	0.738
Management is providing great support in terms of training in digital marketing, and its operations.	3.68	1.144	0.075	0.753
Digital Marketing is cost-effective, easy to implement, and not so high maintenance.	3.66	1.148	0.219	0.744
Management [The use of digital marketing is as per the beliefs of our organization.]	3.75	1.139	0.180	0.747
Management understands the importance of the adoption of digital marketing	3.57	1.282	0.371	0.733
The business environment demands the use of digital marketing	3.64	1.324	0.060	0.757
Competitive advantage is one of the concerns to adopt digital marketing.	3.64	1.328	0.084	0.755
Social network and peer influence motivate to adopt digital marketing in the organization.	3.64	1.330	0.013	0.760
Government schemes, policies, security (different acts, laws) are motivating to adopt digital marketing.	3.63	1.334	-0.014	0.762

Source: Primary Data

Final Draft of the Questionnaire (For Firms)

After purification process and selecting statements of the questionnaire, the final draft of the questionnaire (firms) was prepared. The final draft is prepared by keeping the data relevancy. The Cronbach Alpha value and the mean score values are relevant.

Table 3.7: Final Draft of the Questionnaire (For Firms)

Sr. No.	Factors	Statements	Total
1.	Changing Consumers Attitude	1,2,3,4	4
2.	Organizational Factors	5,6,7,8	4
3.	Technological Factors	9,10,11,12,13	5
4.	Management Factors	14,15,16,17	4
5.	Business Environment Factors	18,19,20,21	4
6.	Challenges in the adoption of Digital Marketing	1,2,3,4,5,6,7,8	8
7.	Effective Modes of Digital Marketing	1,2,3,4,5,6	6
8.	Modes of Digital Marketing Impacting Firm's Sale	1,2,3,4,5	5
9.	Social Media Channels	1,2,3,4,5,6,7	7
		Total	**47**

Source: Primary Data

The table 3.8 contains the part 1 of the questionnaire where there are 21 statements are mentioned which contribute towards the motivating factors in the adoption of digital marketing. The final questionnaire is mentioned in the Annexure 2. Questionnaire is refined many times after seeking comments, suggestions from research experts, industry experts and from the results of reliability analysis.

B. Development of Questionnaire to Study the Customers' Perception Towards Digital Marketing

To study the objective, customers' perception towards digital marketing, different studies like (Shaw and Haynes, 2004), (Ram and Subudhi, 2015), (Tabasum *et al.*, 2014), (Wang and Tang, 2003), (Singhal and Padhmanabhan, 2009), (Dahiya and Gayatri, 2017) etc. have been reviewed on customers' perception and found that there could be different factors to check the customers perception like Online customer relationship, customer reviews, Ease of use, time factors, reliability, advertisement content/message and influencing factors like price of product or services, celebrity endorsement etc. From these identified factors of customer perception, some of the factors used for present study like, ease of use, time factor, influencing factor like Price and celebrity endorsements.

81

Apart from these factors of perception, questionnaire is further categorised in four dimensions like time spent on different platforms, influencing factors, effective modes of digital marketing and effective social media channels by the suggestions of digital marketing and research experts. The data was collected through Likert 5-point scale (1 - strongly disagree & 5 - strongly agree). After the intensive review literature, a preliminary draft of questionnaire for customer was developed (refer to Annexure - II). After developing a preliminary draft, in the next step we have checked the reliability and validity of the questionnaire.

a) Reliability and Validity Analysis

From the alpha value it is very much clear that there is a good inter-relatedness between heterogeneous constructs or statements.

Table 3.8: Reliability Analysis of Factors Associated with Customers' Perception Towards Digital Marketing

Factors	Item Statistics			
	Mean	Std. Deviation	Corrected Item	Cronbach's Alpha
Time spent on digital platforms	2.97	0.799	0.575	0.800
Influencing Factors	3.68	1.190	0.494	0.755
Effective Digital Marketing Modes	3.26	0.996	0.435	0.773
Effective Social Media Channels	3.53	0.762	0.517	0.834

Source: Primary Data

Inter-relatedness between factors is as follows spent time on the internet ($\alpha=0.800$), influencing factors ($\alpha=0.755$), digital marketing modes ($\alpha=0.773$) and social media channels ($\alpha=0.834$). For the purpose of validation, a pilot study is conducted by taking a part of sample having 30 respondents on the 14 statements other than the four factors discussed above.

Table 3.9: Reliability Analysis of Preliminary Questionnaire (Customer)

Reliability Statistics	
Cronbach's Alpha	No. of Items
0.787	14

Source: Primary Data

The value of Cronbach Alpha was 0.787 which is reliable as per the Thumb Rule of Cronbach. So, it is cleared from the calculated value of Cronbach Alpha that our data is reliable and valid for further study. After analysing the reliability & validity of preliminary questionnaire, Final draft of the Questionnaires (Customer) was developed. (Refer to Annexure-IV)

3.9 Limitations of Study

The current study is conducted in a reliable and effective manner but still there are some limitations which are discussed in this section.

- Maximum of the primary data was collected during the Covid-19 period, that has created problems in approaching the repondents.
- Time constraint was one of the major challenge because of the data collection during Covid-19 period.
- As the conditions were not favourable for data collection because of the lockdown situation, some of the data was collected through online modes (Google Form). So it gets difficult to elaborate the things effectively to the respondents online.
- It was a challenge to get the data from the business organisations as many of the respondents were hesitant in sharing the information about their organisation. This may lead to the wrong information if any.
- For the present study, the random sampling method was used in the North region of the country, that may lead to variation in results because of the the sampling region.
- Sample size could also be one of the limitation of the study as for the present study, respondents from the states like Delhi, Haryana, Punjab, Himachal Pradesh of North region were targetted. It is a small portion of the digital marketing users.

These are some of the limitations of present study. But, despite all these limitations, all the necessary measures and precautions have been made to neutralise its impacts on the result outcomes and findings. In this particular chapter, all the research activities or research methods are discussed which are used for present study. In the next chapter the results and discussions are made out on the basis of applied statistical tools and techniques.

Here in this chapter, a discussion is made and presented about the agility of digital marketing, factors motivating the adoption of digital marketing, challenges faced by the companies during the implementation of digital marketing, impact of digital marketing on the business growth and customers' perception about digital marketing. To achieve the different research objectives, collected data was analysed by using different set of statistical tools and techniques. Respondents' profile was analysed and presented by descriptive analysis including frequency and percentages. Data of 420 participants were collected from four business types i.e., Proprietorship firm, Partnership firm, Corporation and Semi-government.

Most of the participants are from healthcare, IT, education, production and manufacturing, food and hospitality, tour & travels, and banking sectors etc. Further, data was also collected from 600 customers, out of which about 580 respond back and 563 responses were found suitable for analysis. Methods like factor analysis, reliability test, correlation, one-way ANOVA, frequency distribution, mean and standard deviation has been adopted to assess the impact of digital marketing on Indian firms. Bar chart and pie charts are used to present data in a graphical form.

4.1 Research Survey and the Framework

The questionnaire was sent to 5 experts for validation. These experts handle different kinds of business such as proprietorship firm, partnership firm, Corporation and semi-government. The basis on their reviews, appropriate changes have been made in the questionnaire and then circulated to the respective people.

Figure 4.1: Response Rate

Response Rate 84%

500 business organisations were approached for data collection but data were received from 450 participants, out of which 30 participants have not completed the survey form. The response rate of the data collection was 84%. The data analysis framework gives a short idea about the work done in this chapter. The data analysis framework is mainly used to structure analytical thinking and also helps in presenting the work systematically (Fray, 2018) (Ferhat Karaca, Paul Graham et al., 2015).

Figure 4.2: Author Designed Framework

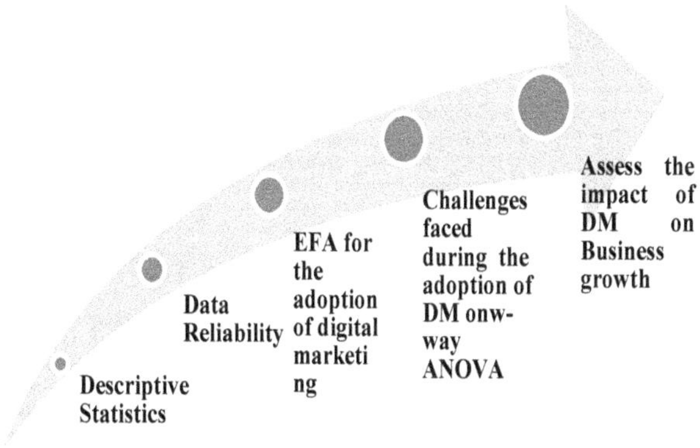

Source: Author Designed Framework

4.2 General Information About the Organizations Employed Digital Marketing

There are various types of organization, out of which only 4 of them have been shortlisted to study the effect of digital marketing in transforming business. The frequency distribution method is adopted to present participants point of view. Categories like type of business, type of industry, digital marketing adoption duration, observe the change in annual revenue after digital marketing adoption, organization-optimized website, etc. have been discussed.

4.2.1 Distribution Based on Type of Business Organizations

Refer to Table 4.1, there are four types of business adopted in the study, and they are as follows sole proprietorship (60%) deduce 252, a partnership firm (10.5%) deduce 44,

Corporation (24.8%) deduce 104, and semi-government (3.8%) deduce 16. The remaining participants (1%) deduce 4 are from another kind of businesses. Hence, most of the participants are from proprietorship firm (60%) and from corporation (24.8%).

Table 4.1: Distribution Based on Type of Business Organisations

Type of business	Frequency	Percentage
Sole Proprietorship	252	60.0%
Partnership	44	10.5%
Corporation	104	24.8%
Semi-Government	16	3.8%
Others	4	1.0%
Total	420	100.0%

Source: Primary Data through Questionnaire

4.2.2 Distribution Based on Industry Type

According to Table 4.2, Industries are generally classified as tertiary, secondary and primary. Secondary industries are further classified as light and heavy.

Table 4.2: Type of Industry

Industry	Frequency	Percentage
Healthcare	80	19.05%
IT Sector	82	19.52%
Legal Industry	6	1.43%
Banking Sector	24	5.71%
BPO	6	1.43%
Hotel and Tourism	32	7.62%
Automobile Sector	20	4.76%
Retail sector	20	4.76%
Production & Manufacturing	40	9.52%
Telecom sector	8	1.90%
Tour and Travels	28	6.67%
Consultancy	8	1.90%
Real Estate	20	4.76%
Education	44	10.48%
Agriculture	2	0.48%
Total	420	100.0%

Source: Primary Data through Questionnaire

For the analysis, there are 15 different industries have been targeted wherein percentage contribution from top five industries are as follows IT sector (19.52%), Healthcare

(19.05%), Education (10.48%), Production & Manufacturing (9.52%) and Hotel and Tourism (7.62%). The remaining sectors who have participated in the survey are as follows Tour and Travels (6.67%), Banking (5.71%), Automobile and Retail (4.76%) each, Real Estate (4.76%), Consultancy (1.90%) and Agriculture (0.48%).

4.2.3 Distribution Based on Duration of Adoption of Digital Marketing

According to Table 4.3, the duration of digital marketing adoption for most participants (60%) deduces 252 is more than 4years, followed by 3to4 years (26.7%) deduce 112, 1-2 years (8.6%) deduce 36 and less than 1 year (4.8%) deduce 20. This infers that most participants, 364 (867%), had adopted digital marketing for more than 3 years.

Table 4.3: Duration of adoption of digital marketing

Duration	Frequency	Percentage
< 1 year	20	4.8%
1 to 2 years	36	8.6%
3 to 4 years	112	26.7%
> 4 years	252	60.0%
Total	420	100.0%

Source: Primary Data through Questionnaire

4.2.4 Distribution Based on Change in Annual Sales Revenue After Adoption of Digital Marketing

Refer to table 4.4, it was found 75.2% deduce 316 participants, said that there is a change in revenue and 3.8% participants deduce 16, found no improvement in their sales.

Table 4.4: Change in annual sale revenue collection after digital marketing adoption

Change in Revenue Collection	Frequency	Percentage
No	16	3.8%
Yes	316	75.2%
Can't Say	88	21.0%
Total	**420**	**100.0%**

Source: Primary Data through Questionnaire

This holds accurate as per the author (S. Andersson, & N. Wikström, 2017). His finding suggested that the effective use of digital marketing improves overall sales and positively affects customer performance, i.e., customer satisfaction, trust, customer referrals, and organizational performance.

4.2.5 Distribution Based on Well Optimized Website of Organization

Regarding having a well-optimized website, 90.5% participants agreed to have a website in place whereas, 9.5% participants denied. As per the report shared by (McGrath, 2019) a well-optimized website is more likely to gain sales and customers. In addition, consumers will also have an opportunity to share the brand details among their network or other social media platforms like Whatsapp, Facebook, Instagram etc.

Table 4.5: Organizations' Profile on the Basis of Well Optimised Website

Organization's Website is Well Optimised	Frequency	Percentage
No	40	9.5%
Yes	380	90.5%
Total	420	100.0%

Source: Primary Data through Questionnaire

4.2.6 Distribution Based on Organizations' Social Media Page

Here from table 4.5 and 4.6, gathered data reveals that 7.1% of businesses don't have a website but have at least a social media page. This infers that companies are aware of the importance of digital marketing in today's environment. According to 97.1% participants, there is a social media page, whereas there is no social media page for 2.9% of businesses.

Table 4.6: Organizations' Profile on the Basis of Social Media Pages

Organizations have Social Media Page	Frequency	Percentage
No	12	2.9%
Yes	408	97.1%
Total	420	100.0%

Source: Primary Data through Questionnaire

4.3 Factors Motivating the Adoption of Digital Marketing

The exploratory factor analysis (EFA) is used to assemble the existing statements based on the measured variables. It is a technique that is used to interpret factors based on the high correlation. Further PCA (Principal Component Analysis) method reduces the statements and forms the factors or components. This type of analysis is mainly used with uncorrelated factors. The main objective of KMO value is to tell us whether the gathered data is suitable for factor analysis or not. This method also helps in telling whether the factors can be extracted from the given statements or not. Here, the number of components extracted by KMO is less.

In table 4.7, based on 21 statements, a correlation matrix has been run to get the determinant value of 0.001. Since the determinant value is greater than 0, this infers that there will not be any computational problems with the given factor analysis.

Further in KMO and Bartlett's Test, KMO value is close to 0.812, with the chi-square value of 2915.609 and a significant value of 0.00 explained in Table 4.8. This infers that, factors affecting digital marketing adoption are substantial in nature, with a KMO value greater than 0.60 (UCLA, 2017). Further, as per the significance rule, the probability value is lesser than 0.05, Bartlett's Test of Sphericity is also found reliable. This considered a relationship between the variables and the rotated matrix where all the matrixes are highly correlated.

Further, Bartlett's test of sphericity helps in assessing whether the correlation matrix is an identity matrix or not. The varimax rotation based on eigenvalues should be greater than 1. Here from the analysis, there are 5 factors found with the cut-off value of 0.490.

Table 4.7: KMO and Bartlett's Test for Motivational Factors Scale

KMO and Bartlett's Test		
Kaiser-Meyer-Olkin Measure of Sampling Adequacy.		0.812
Bartlett's Test of Sphericity	Approx. Chi-Square	2915.609
	Df	210
	Sig.	0.000

Source: Primary Data through Questionnaire

Table 4.8: Correlation Matrix of Motivational Factors Scale for Adoption of Digital Marketing

Correlation Matrix[a]

Statements	CCA-1	CCA-2	CCA-3	CCA-4	Org-1	Org-2	Org-3	Org-4	Tech-1	Tech-2	Tech-3	Tech-4	Tech-5	Mang-1	Mang-2	Mang-3	Mang-4	BE-1	BE-2	BE-3	BE-4
CCA-1	1.0	0.5	0.4	0.3	0.0	0.1	0.2	0.2	-0.1	-0.1	0.0	0.1	-0.1	0.0	0.0	0.0	-0.1	0.0	0.0	-0.1	0.0
CCA-2	0.5	1.0	0.7	0.5	0.1	0.3	0.3	0.3	0.1	0.0	0.0	0.2	0.1	0.1	0.1	0.0	0.1	-0.1	0.0	-0.1	-0.1
CCA-3	0.4	0.7	1.0	0.7	0.2	0.3	0.3	0.4	0.2	0.1	0.0	0.4	0.1	0.1	0.2	0.0	0.2	-0.1	0.0	0.0	0.0
CCA-4	0.3	0.5	0.7	1.0	0.3	0.3	0.2	0.3	0.3	0.2	0.1	0.4	0.1	0.0	0.1	0.0	0.2	-0.1	0.0	-0.1	-0.1
Org-1	0.0	0.1	0.2	0.3	1.0	0.5	0.5	0.5	0.4	0.3	0.3	0.3	0.3	0.0	0.2	0.2	0.4	0.1	0.1	0.0	-0.1
Org-2	0.1	0.3	0.3	0.3	0.5	1.0	0.6	0.7	0.4	0.3	0.2	0.3	0.4	0.0	0.2	0.1	0.2	-0.1	-0.1	-0.1	-0.1
Org-3	0.2	0.3	0.3	0.2	0.5	0.6	1.0	0.7	0.3	0.2	0.1	0.2	0.3	0.0	0.2	0.1	0.2	0.0	-0.1	-0.2	-0.2
Org-4	0.2	0.3	0.4	0.3	0.5	0.7	0.7	1.0	0.4	0.3	0.2	0.3	0.4	0.0	0.2	0.1	0.2	0.0	-0.1	-0.1	0.0
Tech-1	-0.1	0.1	0.2	0.3	0.4	0.4	0.3	0.4	1.0	0.7	0.4	0.5	0.5	0.0	0.2	0.1	0.3	-0.1	-0.1	-0.1	-0.1
Tech-2	-0.1	0.0	0.1	0.2	0.3	0.3	0.2	0.3	0.7	1.0	0.3	0.4	0.4	-0.1	0.1	0.1	0.2	0.0	-0.1	-0.1	-0.1
Tech-3	0.0	0.0	0.0	0.1	0.3	0.2	0.1	0.2	0.4	0.3	1.0	0.3	0.2	0.1	0.1	0.1	0.3	0.0	0.0	0.0	0.0
Tech-4	0.1	0.2	0.4	0.4	0.3	0.3	0.2	0.3	0.5	0.4	0.3	1.0	0.4	-0.1	0.1	0.1	0.2	0.0	-0.1	-0.1	-0.1
Tech-5	-0.1	0.1	0.1	0.1	0.3	0.4	0.3	0.4	0.5	0.4	0.2	0.4	1.0	-0.1	0.1	0.0	0.3	0.0	-0.1	-0.2	-0.2
Mang-1	0.0	0.1	0.1	0.0	0.0	0.0	0.0	0.0	0.0	-0.1	0.1	-0.1	-0.1	1.0	0.2	0.2	0.2	-0.1	0.0	0.1	0.0
Mang-2	0.0	0.1	0.2	0.1	0.2	0.2	0.2	0.2	0.2	0.1	0.1	0.1	0.1	0.2	1.0	0.1	0.2	-0.1	-0.1	-0.1	-0.1
Mang-3	0.0	0.0	0.0	0.0	0.2	0.1	0.1	0.1	0.1	0.1	0.1	0.1	0.0	0.2	0.1	1.0	0.1	0.1	0.1	0.1	0.0
Mang-4	-0.1	0.1	0.2	0.2	0.4	0.2	0.2	0.2	0.3	0.2	0.3	0.2	0.3	0.2	0.2	0.1	1.0	0.1	0.1	0.0	-0.1
BE-1	0.0	-0.1	-0.1	-0.1	0.1	-0.1	0.0	0.0	-0.1	0.0	0.0	0.0	0.0	-0.1	-0.1	0.1	0.1	1.0	0.4	0.3	0.2
BE-2	0.0	0.0	0.0	0.0	0.1	-0.1	-0.1	-0.1	-0.1	-0.1	0.0	-0.1	-0.1	0.0	-0.1	0.1	0.1	0.4	1.0	0.4	0.3
BE-3	-0.1	-0.1	0.0	-0.1	0.0	-0.1	-0.2	-0.1	-0.1	-0.1	0.0	-0.1	-0.2	0.1	-0.1	0.1	0.0	0.3	0.4	1.0	0.4
BE-4	0.0	-0.1	0.0	-0.1	-0.1	-0.1	-0.2	0.0	-0.1	-0.1	0.0	-0.1	-0.2	0.0	-0.1	0.0	-0.1	0.2	0.3	0.4	1.0

Determinant=0.001

Source: Primary Data through Questionnaire

Table 4.9: Total Variance of Motivational Factors Scale

Total Variance Explained						
Comp.	Initial Eigenvalues			Rotation Sums of Squared Loadings		
	Total	% Of Variance	Cumulative %	Total	% Of Variance	Cumulative %
1	4.968	23.658	23.658	2.889	13.756	13.756
2	2.318	11.038	34.696	2.826	13.457	27.213
3	2.059	9.804	44.500	2.698	12.849	40.061
4	1.414	6.736	51.236	2.113	10.064	50.125
5	1.350	6.430	57.666	1.583	7.540	57.666
6	0.968	4.608	62.273			
7	0.901	4.289	66.563			
8	0.835	3.975	70.538			
9	0.798	3.802	74.340			
10	0.732	3.485	77.825			
11	0.639	3.045	80.870			
12	0.612	2.916	83.786			
13	0.554	2.640	86.426			
14	0.515	2.450	88.877			
15	0.426	2.028	90.905			
16	0.412	1.963	92.867			
17	0.384	1.831	94.698			
18	0.327	1.556	96.253			
19	0.302	1.438	97.691			
20	0.267	1.272	98.964			
21	0.218	1.036	100.000			
Extraction Method: Principal Component Analysis.						

Source: Primary Data through Questionnaire

The table 4.9 talked about the total variance explained in the gathered data of 420 participants. As per the results, 57.66% of data could be explained by the 5 identified factors. The Eigen-value of these factors is greater than 1. This table also informs that there are few more motivational factors involved in adopting digital marketing for businesses. This entire process is done via PCA.

Scree Plot

Scree plot is useful in the determination of the factors to retain in Exploratory Factor

Analysis (EFA). It is the graph between eigen values and the number of factors.

Figure 4.1: Scree Plot for Motivational Factors Scale

Scree Plot

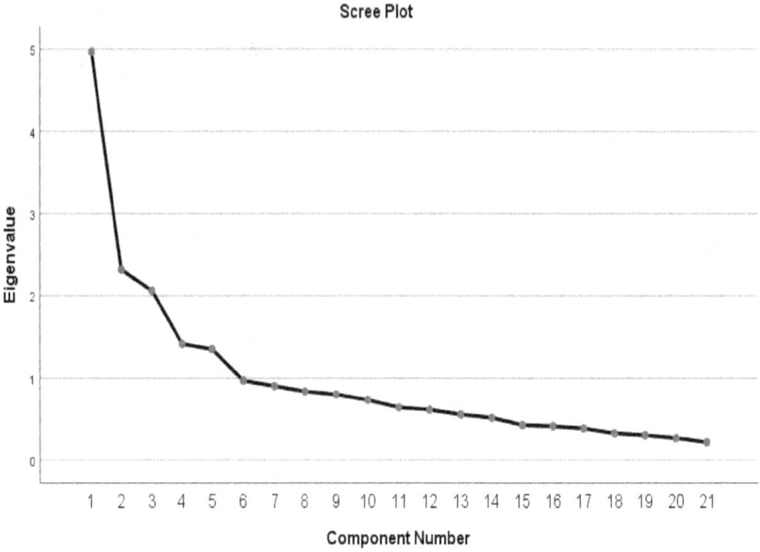

Source: Primary Data through Questionnaire

Table 4.10: Rotated Component Matrix for Motivational Factors Scale

Rotated Component Matrix[a]					
	Components				
Statements	Technological	Organizational	Changing Consumers Attitude	Business Environment	Management
Technological advancements make it convenient to adopt digital marketing	0.812				
Deployment of Artificial Intelligence (AI), chatbots, etc. personalized digital marketing campaigns	0.738				
The adoption of modern technologies reduces the cost of marketing on a digital platform	0.655				
Technological innovations in digital marketing are helpful to increase the effectiveness of promotional and marketing activities on a digital platform	0.574				
Data management is not a challenge in the adoption of digital marketing	0.511				

Digital Marketing is becoming a part of the workstyle due to the continued dominance of the internet and technology	0.817			
With the use of digital marketing tools, the productivity of the organization has increased	0.798			
Advanced technological infrastructure in an organization encourages to adopt digital marketing	0.735			
The availability of financial resources makes it possible for the organization to adopt digital marketing	0.648			
Consumers' preference has changed from traditional media (TV, radio, newspaper, etc.) to digital media (blogs, social media, website, apps, etc.)		0.843		
Customers find it convenient to interact through Digital Marketing.		0.820		
More customized messages can be communicated through digital marketing.		0.740		
Customers are spending sufficient time over the internet because it is easy to access.		0.650		
Competitive advantage is one of the concerns to adopt digital marketing.			0.770	
Social network and peer influence motivate to adopt digital marketing in the Organization			0.725	
The business environment demands the use of digital marketing			0.659	
Government schemes, policies, security (different acts, laws) are motivating to adopt digital marketing			0.619	
Management is providing great support in terms of training in digital marketing, and its operations				0.758
Digital Marketing is cost-effective, easy to implement, and not so high maintenance				0.553
Management understands the importance of the adoption of digital marketing				0.518
The use of digital marketing is as per the beliefs of our organization				0.476
Extraction Method: Principal Component Analysis. Rotation Method: Varimax with Kaiser Normalization.[a]				
a. Rotation converged in 6 iterations.				

Source: Primary Data through Questionnaire

Here rotated component matrix (RCM) is used to group factors or components through the varimax rotation method. The table demonstrated below represents the factor loading at statement level with the cut off of 0.419. Therefore, there are no cross-loadings observed or present in the analysis of 21 statements.

The five identified statements are as follows Technological (65.8%), Organizational (75%), Changing Consumers Attitude (76.3%), Business Environment (69.3%) and Management (57.6%).

4.3.1 Interpretation of the Extracted Groups

So far, on the basis of correlation analysis, 5 factors with 21 statements were identified that motivate adoption of digital marketing. In table 4.11, these 5 factors were found significant (significance values within the tolerance limit of 0.05) and reliable (Cronbach alpha is greater than the tolerance limit of 0.70).

Table 4.11: Significance of Extracted Motivational Factors

Factors	Factor Loading	Reliability	Sig	Rank
Technological Factor	65.8%	0.76	0.000	4
Organizational Factor	75.0%	0.84	0.000	2
Changing Consumers Attitude	76.3%	0.80	0.052	1
Business Environment Factor	69.3%	0.77	0.010	3
Management Factor	57.6%	0.74	0.008	5

Source: Primary Data through Questionnaire

Refer to table 4.11, It can be seen that for Changing Consumers Attitude, the values of factor loading and Cronbach alpha are 76.3% & 0.80 respectively. One the basis of these value it can be said that Changing Consumers Attitude is the most significant and ranked first among all 5 **motivational factors in adoption of digital marketing**. (Tortorice, 2017), only extraordinary and worth sharing advertisement are visible to most of shoppers on digital platform. A good and creative ad will significantly increase brand awareness and sale.

The second important factor is the organizational factor, with a factor loading of 75.0% and an alpha value of 0.84. This factor has shown an excellent internal consistency among the statements. As per the (Lee, 2021), in today's time, digital marketing has completely replaced traditional marketing wherein organizations can't ignore the prerequisite of a digital marketing strategy because of being faster, effective, and cheaper than the old style of marketing.

The third factor is the business environment, with a factor loading of 69.3%. The alpha value is close to 0.77. As per the participants, areas like competitive advantage (factor loading: 77%), social network and peer influence (factor loading: 72.5%), the demand of the use of digital marketing (factor loading: 65.9%) and government schemes, policies, security (different acts, laws) (factor loading: 61.9%) are the influential factors to promote the product sale in the new digital age. This could only be possible through the adoption of digital marketing.

The fourth factor is technological, with the factor loading of 65.8% and an alpha value of 0.76. Once the business need is clear, organizations are steeping towards the technical requirement of fulfilling the end goal. As per the participants, for businesses, advancement in technology help them in the adoption of digital marketing (factor loading: 81.2%), deployment of artificial intelligence (AI), chatbots, etc. personalized digital marketing campaign (factor loading: 73.8%), adoption of modern technologies reduces the cost of marketing on a digital platform (factor loading: 65.5%), technology innovations helps in increasing the effectiveness of promotional and marketing activities (factor loading: 57.4%) and data management (factor loading: 51.1%).

Figure 4.2: Motivational Factors in Adoption of Digital Marketing

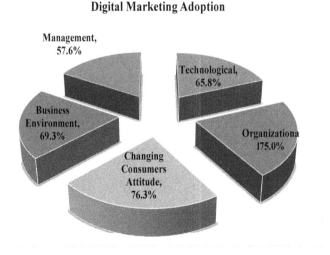

Source: Primary Data Through Questionnaire

The fifth and last factor is management factor, with a factor loading of 57.6% and an alpha value of 0.74. As per the participant, management provides excellent support in training digital marketing (factor loading: 0.758) because this is cost-effective and easy to implement with high maintenance (factor loading: 0.553). Participants further said that organizations do understand the importance of the adoption of digital marketing   (factor   loading: 0.518). Here the understanding is based on the belief of getting good returns from digital marketing (factor loading: 0.476).

Hence overall, it can be said that these identified factors are motivating the adoption of digital marketing. **(H_1^1 is accepted)**

4.4 Challenges Faced by Firms in the Adoption of Digital Marketing

The adoption of digital marketing comes with some challenges, and these challenges help businesses to realize their true potential (V. Kumar, S. Sunder, A. Sharma, 2015). Here in the study, there are a couple of challenges identified, wherein participants have shared their point of view regarding the identified motivating factors of digital marketing. Mean values have been calculated to present participants responses. Data collected in the 5-points Likert scale, wherein 1 stand for strongly disagree and 5 stands for strongly agree.

Table 4.12: Descriptive Statistics of Challenges Faced in Adoption of Digital Marketing

Sr. No.	Challenges	Mean	Standard Deviation
1.	Data Management	4.06	0.86
2.	Customers'/Employees' Changing Experience	3.86	1.22
3.	Selection of Right Technology	3.81	1.17
4.	Strategy Development	3.78	1.09
5.	Lack of Finance	3.76	1.11
6.	Training of Team Staff	3.65	1.19
7.	Competition Analysis	3.64	1.21
8.	Government Policies	3.23	1.37

Source: Primary Data Through Questionnaire

Table 4.12 shows the descriptive statistics of the challenges faced by the business organisations in the adoption of digital marketing. From the table it is clear that the mean value of the challenge Data Management is the highest (4.06) among all followed by

Customers' and Employees' Changing Behaviour (3.86), Selection of right technology (3.81), Strategy Development (3.78), Lack of Finance (3.76), Training of team/Staff (3.65), Competition Analysis (3.64), Government Policies (3.23). From this data, it is clear that Data Management is the biggest challenge for organisations in the adoption of digital marketing, followed by changing behaviour of consumers and employees and they consider Government Policies as the least faced challenge.

Figure 4.3: Mean Values of Different Identified Challenges

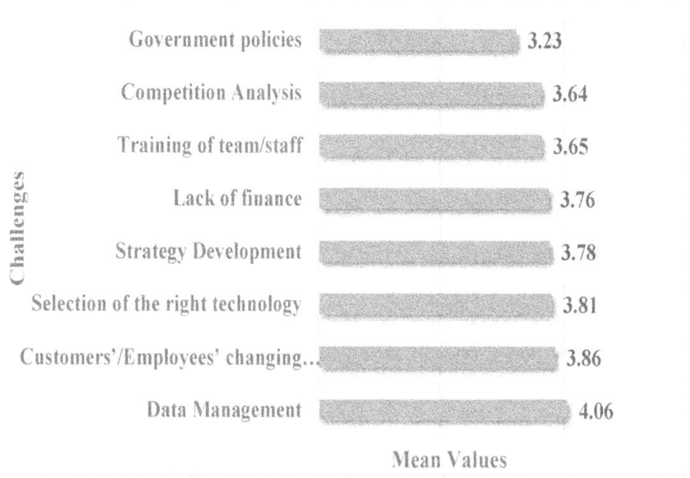

Source: Primary Data Through Questionnaire

Further to understand the significance level of the challenges or problems faced by the firm during adoption or implementation of digital marketing below-listed hypothesis has been formed.

Hypothesis: $H_1{}^2$: There is a significance difference between Challenges faced by the firms and Factor Motivates the adoption of digital marketing.

Here, one-way ANOVA is used to assess the significance level of the challenges faced by firms at the motivational level during the adoption of digital marketing. Since both the parameters (challenges and motivational factors) are parametric in nature, one-way ANOVA is adopted. Here F-value and significance value is observed while interpreting the results at 95% confidence level. All the respective tables of One-way ANOVA are demonstrated below for the discussion.

4.4.2 Significance of Identified Challenges with "Changing Consumers Attitude"

In changing consumers attitude, out of 8 challenges, seven of them are significant. The f-value and the significant value of these challenges are as follows data management (f-value: 2.450, sig=0.046, ≤0.05), identification and selection of the right technology (f-value: 2.463, sig=0.045, ≤0.05), customers' changing experience (f-value:5.595, sig= 0.000, ≤0.05), development of digital marketing strategy (f-value: 3.403, sig=0.009, ≤0.05), analysis of the competition (f-value: 5.648, sig: 0.000, ≤0.05), lack of finance (f-value: 3.133, sig: 0.015, ≤0.05), and government policies (f-value: 4.434, sig= 0.002, ≤0.05).

Table 4.13: Significance of Identified Challenges with "Changing Consumers Attitude"

Changing Consumers Attitude – ANOVA							
Challenges		Sum of Squares	Df	Mean Square	F	Sig.	Result
Data Management	Between Groups	7.217	4	1.804	2.450	0.046	
	Within Groups	305.631	415	0.736			Significant
	Total	312.848	419				
Identification and Selection of the right technology	Between Groups	13.507	4	3.377	2.463	0.045	
	Within Groups	569.055	415	1.371			Significant
	Total	582.562	419				
Training of team/staff	Between Groups	1.448	4	0.362	0.259	0.904	
	Within Groups	580.114	415	1.398			Not Significant
	Total	581.562	419				
Customers 'changing experience	Between Groups	31.982	4	7.995	5.595	0.000	
	Within Groups	593.009	415	1.429			Significant
	Total	624.990	419				
Development of digital marketing strategy	Between Groups	15.766	4	3.942	3.403	0.009	
	Within Groups	480.624	415	1.158			Significant
	Total	496.390	419				
Analysis of the competition	Between Groups	31.844	4	7.961	5.648	0.000	
	Within Groups	584.963	415	1.410			Significant
	Total	616.807	419				
Lack of finance	Between Groups	15.233	4	3.808	3.133	0.015	
	Within Groups	504.508	415	1.216			Significant
	Total	519.740	419				
Government policies	Between Groups	32.024	4	8.006	4.434	0.002	
	Within Groups	749.259	415	1.805			Significant
	Total	781.283	419				

Source: Primary Data Through Questionnaire

There is only one statement such as training of team/ staff which doesn't find to be significant this could be because staff training is not related as consumer attitude. The f-value of the team training is 0.259, and the significant value is 0.904, greater than the tolerance limit of 0.05. The degree of freedom of the data between groups is close to 4, and with-in groups is close to 415. The total number of participants for the survey was 420; hence overall degree of freedom is close to 419 (n-1). Therefore, challenges faced in adopting digital technology are significant at changing consumers' attitude level.

4.4.2 Significance of Identified Challenges with Organizational Factors

With organizational factor, out of 8 challenges, four of them are significant. The f-value and the significant value of these challenges are as follows data management (f-value: 7.685, sig=0.000, ≤0.05), identification and selection of the right technology (f-value: 9.912, sig=0.000, ≤0.05), training or team/ staff (f-value: 9.751, sig= 0.000, ≤0.05), and customers' changing experience (f-value: 26.112, sig= 0.000, ≤0.05).

There are four statements such as the development of digital marketing strategy, analysis of the competition, lack of finance, and government policies which doesn't found to be significant. This could be because factors like organization productivity, advanced technology infrastructure, and financial resources have been considered; there are different types of challenges. That is why the remaining challenges are not found significant as per the participants.

The significant value for all the listed four challenges is greater than 0.05. The degree of freedom of the data between groups is close to 4, and with-in groups is close to 415. The total number of participants for the survey was 420; hence overall degree of freedom is close to 419 (n-1). Therefore, challenges faced in adopting digital technology are partially significant at organizational behaviour. The F values with mean square value and some of square are discussed in the table below. Four challenges named development of digital marketing strategy, lack of finance, analysis of competition and government policies are found insignificant.

Table 4.14: Significance of Identified Challenges with Organizational Factors

Challenges		Sum of Squares	df	Mean Square	F	Sig.	Result
Organizational – ANOVA							
Data Management	Between Groups	21.576	4	5.394	7.685	0.000	Significant
	Within Groups	291.272	415	0.702			
	Total	312.848	419				
Identification and Selection of the right technology	Between Groups	50.802	4	12.700	9.912	0.000	Significant
	Within Groups	531.760	415	1.281			
	Total	582.562	419				
Training of team/staff	Between Groups	49.962	4	12.491	9.751	0.000	Significant
	Within Groups	531.599	415	1.281			
	Total	581.562	419				
Customers changing experience	Between Groups	125.668	4	31.417	26.112	0.000	Significant
	Within Groups	499.322	415	1.203			
	Total	624.990	419				
Development of digital marketing strategy	Between Groups	1.217	4	0.304	0.255	0.907	Not Significant
	Within Groups	495.174	415	1.193			
	Total	496.390	419				
Analysis of the competition	Between Groups	5.425	4	1.356	0.921	0.452	Not Significant
	Within Groups	611.382	415	1.473			
	Total	616.807	419				
Lack of finance	Between Groups	2.610	4	0.652	0.524	0.718	Not Significant
	Within Groups	517.131	415	1.246			
	Total	519.740	419				
Government policies	Between Groups	9.082	4	2.271	1.220	0.302	Not Significant
	Within Groups	772.201	415	1.861			
	Total	781.283	419				

Source: Primary Data through Questionnaire

4.4.3 Significance of Identified Challenges with Technological Factors

In technology, out of 8 challenges, four of them are significant. The f-value and the significant value of these challenges are as follows:

Table 4.15: Significance of Identified Challenges with Technological Factors

Technological Factors – ANOVA							
Challenges		Sum of Squares	df	Mean Square	F	Sig.	Result
Data Management	Between Groups	20.261	4	5.065	7.184	0.000	
	Within Groups	292.587	415	0.705			Significant
	Total	312.848	419				
Identification and Selection of the right technology	Between Groups	61.097	4	15.274	12.156	0.000	
	Within Groups	521.465	415	1.257			Significant
	Total	582.562	419				
Training of team/staff	Between Groups	65.343	4	16.336	13.133	0.000	
	Within Groups	516.219	415	1.244			Significant
	Total	581.562	419				
Customers' changing experience	Between Groups	78.989	4	19.747	15.009	0.000	
	Within Groups	546.001	415	1.316			Significant
	Total	624.990	419				
Development of digital marketing strategy	Between Groups	2.471	4	0.618	0.519	0.722	Not Significant
	Within Groups	493.919	415	1.190			
	Total	496.390	419				
Analysis of the competition	Between Groups	12.108	4	3.027	2.077	0.083	Not Significant
	Within Groups	604.699	415	1.457			
	Total	616.807	419				
Lack of finance	Between Groups	5.202	4	1.300	1.049	0.382	Not Significant
	Within Groups	514.539	415	1.240			
	Total	519.740	419				
Government policies	Between Groups	5.481	4	1.370	0.733	0.570	Not Significant
	Within Groups	775.803	415	1.869			
	Total	781.283	419				

Source: Primary Data through Questionnaire

data management (f-value: 7.184, sig=0.000, ≤0.05), identification and selection of the right technology (f-value: 12.156, sig=0.000, ≤0.05), training or team/ staff (f-value: 13.133, sig= 0.000, ≤0.05), and customers' changing experience (f-value: 15.009, sig= 0.000, ≤0.05). There are four statements such as the development of digital marketing strategy, analysis of the competition, lack of finance, and government policies which doesn't found to be significant.

This could be because in technology factors like technology advancements, deployment of artificial intelligence (AI), chatbots, etc. personalized digital marketing campaigns, adoption of modern technologies, technology innovations, etc., have been considered. There are different types of challenges faced by technology while adopting digital marketing. That is why the remaining challenges are not found significant as per the participants. The significant value for all the listed four challenges is greater than 0.05. The degree of freedom of the data between groups is close to 4, and with-in groups is close to 415.

The total number of participants for the survey was 420; hence overall degree of freedom is close to 419 (n-1). Therefore, challenges faced in adopting digital technology are partially significant to technology. The F values with mean square value and some of square are discussed in the table below. Four challenges named development of digital marketing strategy, lack of finance, analysis of competition and government policies are found insignificant. That means the other challenges like data management, identification of right technology etc, are found significant.

4.4.4 Significance of Identified Challenges with Management Factor

In management, out of 8 challenges, six of them are significant. The f-value and the significant value of these challenges are as follows data management (f-value: 0.205, sig=0.036, ≤0.05), identification and selection of the right technology (f-value: 3.552, sig=0.007, ≤0.05), training of team/ staff (f-value: 2.538, sig=0.040, ≤0.05), customers' changing experience (f-value: 2.757, sig= 0.028, ≤0.05), analysis of the competition (f-value: 0.529, sig: 0.014, ≤0.05), and government policies (f-value: 0.593, sig= 0.007, ≤0.05). There are two challenges, such as lack of finance and the development of digital marketing strategy, which doesn't find to be significant. This is strange because in management, challenges like managing finance and developing marketing strategy are also the fundamental challenges faced by the firms. The f-values of these two factors are 0.778 & 0.330, and the significant value is 0.540 & 0.857, greater than the tolerance limit of 0.05.

Table 4.16: Significance of Identified Challenges with Management Factor

Management- ANOVA						
Challenges		**Sum of Squares**	**df**	**Mean Square**	**F**	**Sig.**	**Result**
Data Management	Between Groups	0.616	4	0.154	0.205	0.036	Significant
	Within Groups	312.232	415	0.752			
	Total	312.848	419				
Identification and Selection of the right technology	Between Groups	19.282	4	4.821	3.552	0.007	Significant
	Within Groups	563.280	415	1.357			
	Total	582.562	419				
Training of team/staff	Between Groups	13.885	4	3.471	2.538	0.040	Significant
	Within Groups	567.677	415	1.368			
	Total	581.562	419				
Customers' changing experience	Between Groups	16.181	4	4.045	2.757	0.028	Significant
	Within Groups	608.810	415	1.467			
	Total	624.990	419				
Development of digital marketing strategy	Between Groups	1.576	4	0.394	0.330	0.857	Not Significant
	Within Groups	494.814	415	1.192			
	Total	496.390	419				
Analysis of the competition	Between Groups	3.132	4	0.783	0.529	0.014	Significant
	Within Groups	613.675	415	1.479			
	Total	616.807	419				
Lack of finance	Between Groups	3.868	4	0.967	0.778	0.540	Not Significant
	Within Groups	515.873	415	1.243			
	Total	519.740	419				
Government policies	Between Groups	4.439	4	1.110	0.593	0.007	Significant
	Within Groups	776.844	415	1.872			
	Total	781.283	419				

Source: Primary Data through Questionnaire

Therefore, challenges faced in adopting digital technology are significant at the management level. The F values with mean square value and some of square are discussed in the table 4.16 below. Two challenges named development of digital marketing strategy; lack of finance is found insignificant.

4.4.5 Significance of Identified Challenges with Business Environment Factor

With the business environment, out of 8 challenges, seven of them are significant. The f-value and the significant value of these challenges are as

Table 4.17: Significance of Identified Challenges with Business Environment Factor

Challenges		Sum of Squares	df	Mean Square	F	Sig.	Result
Business Environment – ANOVA							
Data Management	Between Groups	6.022	4	1.505	2.036	0.089	Not Significant
	Within Groups	306.826	415	0.739			
	Total	312.848	419				
Identification and Selection of the right technology	Between Groups	13.558	4	3.389	2.472	0.044	Significant
	Within Groups	569.004	415	1.371			
	Total	582.562	419				
Training of team/staff	Between Groups	11.554	4	2.888	2.103	0.008	Significant
	Within Groups	570.008	415	1.374			
	Total	581.562	419				
Customers' changing experience	Between Groups	13.623	4	3.406	2.312	0.051	Significant
	Within Groups	611.368	415	1.473			
	Total	624.990	419				
Development of digital marketing strategy	Between Groups	1.830	4	0.457	0.384	0.008	Significant
	Within Groups	494.561	415	1.192			
	Total	496.390	419				
Analysis of the competition	Between Groups	10.972	4	2.743	1.879	0.011	Significant
	Within Groups	605.835	415	1.460			
	Total	616.807	419				
Lack of finance	Between Groups	2.345	4	0.586	0.470	0.008	Significant
	Within Groups	517.396	415	1.247			
	Total	519.740	419				
Government policies	Between Groups	3.795	4	0.949	0.506	0.007	Significant
	Within Groups	777.489	415	1.873			
	Total	781.283	419				

Source: Primary Data through Questionnaire

follows the development of digital marketing strategy (f-value: 0.384, sig=0.008, ≤0.05), identification and selection of the right technology (f-value: 2.472, sig=0.044, ≤0.05), training of team/ staff (f-value: 2.130, sig=0.008, ≤0.05), customers' changing experience (f-value: 2.312, sig= 0.051, ≤0.05), analysis of the competition (f-value: 1.879, sig: 0.011, ≤0.05), lack of finance (f-value: 0.470, sig= 0.008, ≤0.05), and government policies (f-value: 0.506, sig= 0.007, ≤0.05). There is only one challenge, such as data management, which is not found significant. This could be because, in the business environment, data management doesn't play much significant role. The f-value of this factor is 2.036, and the significant value is 0.089, greater than the tolerance limit of 0.05. The degree of freedom of the data between groups is close to 4, and with-in groups is close to 415. Table 4.18 is showing the significance of the identified challenges with overall motivational factors.

Table 4.18: Significance of Identified Challenges with Overall Motivational Factors

Factors of Digital Marketing Adoption	Values	Challenges							
		Data Management	Identification and selection of the right technology	Training of team/staff	Customers' changing experience	Development of digital marketing strategy	Analysis of the competition	Lack of finance	Government policies
CCA	F	2.45	2.46	0.26	5.60	3.40	5.65	3.13	4.43
	Sig.	0.05	0.04	**0.90**	0.00	0.01	0.00	0.01	0.00
Org.	F	7.69	9.91	9.75	26.11	0.25	0.92	0.52	1.22
	Sig.	0.00	0.00	0.00	0.00	0.91	**0.45**	**0.72**	**0.30**
Tech.	F	7.18	12.16	13.13	15.01	0.52	2.08	1.05	0.73
	Sig.	0.00	0.00	0.00	0.00	**0.72**	0.08	**0.38**	**0.57**
Mang.	F	0.20	3.55	2.54	2.76	0.33	0.53	0.78	0.59
	Sig.	0.04	0.01	0.04	0.03	**0.86**	0.01	0.54	0.01
BE	F	2.04	2.47	2.10	2.31	0.38	1.88	0.47	0.51
	Sig.	0.09	0.04	0.01	0.05	0.01	0.01	0.01	0.01

Source: Primary Data through Questionnaire

(Where Changing Consumers Attitude = CCA, Organizational = Org., Technological = Tech, Management = Mang., Business Environment = BE)

Therefore, at the overall level, there is a synergy in the combined effect of two parameters i.e., motivational factors and the challenges faced in adopting digital marketing. Hence, it can be concluded that the firms face challenges or problems during the adoption of digital marketing and there is a significance between the identified challenges and the motivational factors in the adoption of digital marketing. Hence our hypothesis H_1^2 **is accepted.**

4.5 Impact of Digital Marketing on the Sale of Business Organisations

In the new era, a technology-based approach has left a significant impact on the business style. This approach has some characteristics and dynamics that need to be understood and implemented for effective marketing strategic initiatives. Various research scholars have articulated multiple classifications of digital channels. As per (Mohammed T. Nuseir et al., 2020), from the 20th century, digitalization has become a crucial part of any business, where the evolving trend of digital media utilization has transformed the business competition and the way of the consumer behaviour attitude.

Table 4.19: Impact of Digital Marketing on Sale of Business Organizations

Statements	Disagree Number (%)	Neutral Number (%)	Agree Number (%)
The adoption of digital marketing has increased the sale of our business.	24 (5.7%)	24 (5.7%)	372 (88.6%)
I received more orders after the adoption of digital marketing.	24 (5.7%)	40 (9.5%)	356 (84.8%)
My sale revenue has not affected after the adoption of digital marketing.	68 (16.2%)	60 (14.3%)	292 (69.5%)
I have received more queries from buyers of my products in the market.	16 (3.8%)	52 (12.4%)	352 (83.8%)
My customer base has been increased after opting digital marketing.	16 (3.8%)	64 (15.2%)	340 (81.0%)

Source: Primary Data through Questionnaire

The further author added that digitalization does impact business and influence brand and product marketing through the various channels like Social Media Marketing (SMM),

Google Ads/Search Engine Marketing (SEM), Email Marketing (EM), Search Engine Optimization (SEO), Content Marketing (CM), and Affiliate Marketing (AM). Several works of literature have addressed the specific need of a market in the digital world. The online accessibility of services & goods enables companies to search, enquire, interact, complain, purchase and pay from remote locations. This has made life convenient for sellers and buyers. Digital marketing has also generated a lot of jobs because of the excessive use of the requirement. As per (Lee, 2021), most firms have adopted technological equipment & systems for effective interaction with the consumers. Nowadays, in companies, most marketing strategies are significantly inclined towards the espousal of online interactive systems to efficiently share information.

Figure 4.4: Impact of Digital Marketing on Sale of Business Organizations

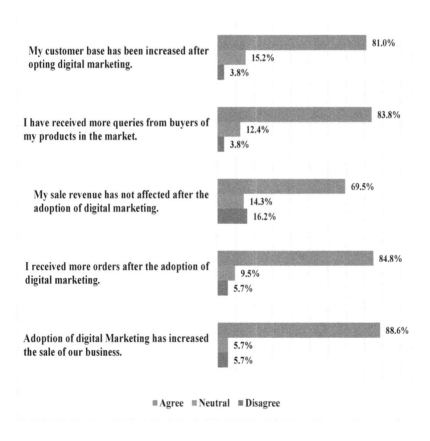

Source: Primary Data through Questionnaire

This section is talking about the impact of digital marketing on sales of business firms. As per the gathered data, the adoption of digital marketing has increased business sale (88.6%). Post digitization, business started receiving more orders (84.8%). The sale revenue has grown up by (69.5%). There are more queries from the product buyers (83.8%), and there is an increase in the customer database (81.0%). Overall, there is an impact observed as per the firms and the participants. Further, to understand the significance level of the impact of digital marketing on the business sale compared with the digital marketing modes, below-listed hypothesis has been formed. We have also studied he correlation between overall sale increase and various modes of digital marketing. this corelation is presented in table 4.20.

Table 4.20: Correlation of Sale Growth with the Various Modes of Digital Marketing

Correlations							
Correlations		AM	SMM	SEM	EM	SEO	EM
Overall Sale Growth	Pearson Correlation	$.412^{**}$	$.546^{**}$	$.289^{**}$	0.042	0.081	$.223^{**}$
	Sig. (2-tailed)	0.000	0.000	0.000	0.393	0.096	0.000
	N	420	420	420	420	420	420
**. Correlation is significant at the 0.01 level (2-tailed).							

Source: Primary Data through Questionnaire

Where: Social Media Marketing: SMM, Google Ads/Search Engine Marketing: SEM, Email Marketing: EM, Search Engine Optimization: SEO, Content Marketing: CM, Affiliate Marketing: AM. Here, as per the participants, sales growth via e-mail marketing has shown the weakest correlation of 4.2%, whereas Social Media Marketing has demonstrated the highest correlation of 54.6%, followed by Affiliate Marketing (41.2%). Following hypothesis ($H_1{}^3$) was formulated in the present research. Here, one-way ANOVA is used to assess the significance level of the impact of digital marketing modes on business growth at various platforms of social media, where digital marketing modes are the dependent variable and social media platforms are the independent variables. Since both the parameters are parametric in nature, that is why one-way ANOVA is adopted. Here F-value and significance value is observed while interpreting the results at 95% confidence level. All the respective tables of One-way ANOVA are demonstrated below for the discussion.

Hypothesis: H_1^3: There is significant impact of various modes of digital marketing on sale of business organization. In support of above hypothesis following sub-hypothesis were framed: **Hypothesis:** $H_1^{3.1}$: There is significant impact of Social Media Marketing on sale of business organization.

Table 4.21: Significance of Social Media Marketing with Sale of Business

ANOVA						
Statements		**Sum of Squares**	**Df**	**Mean Square**	**F**	**Sig.**
The adoption of Digital Marketing has increased the sale of our business.	Between Groups	212.388	4	53.097	97.299	0.000
	Within Groups	226.470	415	0.546		
	Total	438.857	419			
I received more orders after the adoption of Digital Marketing	Between Groups	220.161	4	55.040	107.324	0.000
	Within Groups	212.829	415	0.513		
	Total	432.990	419			
My sale revenue has not affected after the adoption of Digital Marketing	Between Groups	76.498	4	19.124	12.215	0.000
	Within Groups	649.750	415	1.566		
	Total	726.248	419			
I have received more queries from buyers of my products in the market.	Between Groups	89.933	4	22.483	40.197	0.000
	Within Groups	232.124	415	0.559		
	Total	322.057	419			
My customer base has been increased after opting for Digital Marketing.	Between Groups	135.645	4	33.911	62.032	0.000
	Within Groups	226.869	415	0.547		
	Total	362.514	419			

Source: Primary Data through Questionnaire

Table 4.20 represents significance of social media marketing on sale of business organization. The f-values for the adoption of digital marketing has increased the sale of our business (f-value: 97.299, sig=0.000, ≤0.05), received more orders (f-value: 107.324, sig=0.000, ≤0.05), increased in sale revenue (f-value: 12.215, sig=0.000, ≤0.05), have started receiving more queries from buyers (f-value: 40.197, sig=0.000, ≤0.05), and increase in customer base (f-value: 62.032, sig=0.000, ≤0.05) were found significant.

Therefore, it can be concluded that through SMM has significant impact on sale of business organization. This result is matched with previous research works like (Khadije Abdipour et al., 2019), there is a significant growth observed in business in 2018 due to the adoption of social media marketing. In addition, the author said that reaching mass consumers at a low cost has become possible through the online SMM medium. For more sales, businesses should productively use SMM and have innovative campaigns to reach their respective customers.

Therefore, it can be said that Hypothesis: $H_1^{3.1}$: There is significant impact of social media marketing on sale of business organization/for business growth is accepted.

4.5.2 Google Ads/Search Engine Marketing

Hypothesis: $H_1^{3.2}$: There is significant impact of Search Engine Marketing on sale of business organization.

In search engine marketing, out of 5 factors responsible for sale growth, all of them are significant. The f-value and the significant value of these factors are as follows the adoption of search engine marketing has increased business sale (f-value: 149.464, sig=0.000, ≤0.05), received more orders (f-value: 107.407, sig=0.000, ≤0.05), increased in sale revenue (f-value: 25.126, sig=0.000, ≤0.05), have started receiving more queries from buyers (f-value: 40.197, sig=0.000, ≤0.05), and increase in customer base (f-value: 39.426, sig=0.000, ≤0.05). The degree of freedom of the data between groups is close to 4, and with-in groups is close to 415. The total number of participants for the survey was 420; hence overall degree of freedom is close to 419 (n-1). Therefore, it can be concluded that through SEM, there is an impact in business sales and customer acquisition.

Table 4.22: Significance of Search Engine Marketing with Sale of Business

ANOVA						
Statements		Sum of Squares	Df	Mean Square	F	Sig.
The adoption of Digital Marketing has increased the sale of our business.	Between Groups	259.043	4	64.761	149.464	0.000
	Within Groups	179.814	415	0.433		
	Total	438.857	419			
I received more orders after the adoption of Digital Marketing	Between Groups	220.245	4	55.061	107.407	0.000
	Within Groups	212.746	415	0.513		
	Total	432.990	419			
My sale revenue has not affected after the adoption of Digital Marketing.	Between Groups	141.589	4	35.397	25.126	0.000
	Within Groups	584.659	415	1.409		
	Total	726.248	419			
I have received more queries from buyers of my products in the market.	Between Groups	88.684	4	22.171	39.426	0.000
	Within Groups	233.373	415	0.562		
	Total	322.057	419			
My customer base has been increased after opting for Digital Marketing.	Between Groups	119.642	4	29.911	51.109	0.000
	Within Groups	242.872	415	0.585		
	Total	362.514	419			

Source: Primary Data through Questionnaire

4.5.3 E-mail Marketing

Hypothesis: $H_1^{3.3}$: There is significant impact of Email Marketing on sale of business organization/for business growth.

In e-mail marketing, out of 5 factors responsible for sale growth, all of them are significant. The f-value and the significant value of these factors are as follows the adoption of email marketing has increased business sale (f-value: 47.920, sig=0.000, ≤0.05), received more orders (f-value: 54.249, sig=0.000, ≤0.05), increased in sale revenue (f-value: 5.584, sig=0.000, ≤0.05), have started receiving more queries from buyers (f-value: 24.538, sig=0.000, ≤0.05), and increase in customer base (f-value: 29.548, sig=0.000, ≤0.05). The degree of freedom of the data between groups is close to 4, and with-in groups is close to 415. The total number of participants for the survey was 420; hence overall degree of freedom is close to 419 (n-1). Therefore, it can be concluded that through EM, there is an impact in business sales and customer acquisition.

Table 4.23: Significance of Email Marketing with Sale of Business

ANOVA						
		Sum of Squares	df	Mean Square	F	Sig.
The adoption of Digital Marketing has increased the sale of our business.	Between Groups	138.657	4	34.664	47.920	0.000
	Within Groups	300.200	415	0.723		
	Total	438.857	419			
I received more orders after the adoption of Digital Marketing.	Between Groups	148.668	4	37.167	54.249	0.000
	Within Groups	284.322	415	0.685		
	Total	432.990	419			
My sale revenue has not affected after the adoption of Digital Marketing.	Between Groups	37.092	4	9.273	5.584	0.000
	Within Groups	689.156	415	1.661		
	Total	726.248	419			
I have received more queries from buyers of my products in the market.	Between Groups	61.602	4	15.400	24.538	0.000
	Within Groups	260.456	415	0.628		
	Total	322.057	419			
My customer base has been increased after opting for Digital Marketing.	Between Groups	80.359	4	20.090	29.548	0.000
	Within Groups	282.156	415	0.680		
	Total	362.514	419			

Source: Primary Data through Questionnaire

4.5.4 Search Engine Optimization

Hypothesis: $H_1^{3.4}$: There is significant impact of Search Engine Optimization on sale of business organisation.

Out of 5 factors responsible for sale growth in search engine optimization marketing, all of them are significant. The f-value and the significant value of these factors are as follows the adoption of search engine optimization has increased business sale (f-value: 116.457, sig=0.000, ≤0.05), received more orders (f-value: 112.467, sig=0.000, ≤0.05), increased in sale revenue (f-value: 15.602, sig=0.000, ≤0.05), have started receiving more queries from buyers (f-value: 21.425, sig=0.000, ≤0.05), and increase in customer base (f-value: 34.335, sig=0.000, ≤0.05). The degree of freedom of the data between groups is close to 4, and within groups is close to 415. The total number of participants for the survey was 420; hence overall degree of freedom is close to 419 (n-1). Therefore, it can be concluded that through SEO, there is an impact in business sales and customer acquisition.

Table 4.24: Significance of Search Engine Optimization with Sale of Business

ANOVA						
Statements		**Sum of Squares**	**df**	**Mean Square**	**F**	**Sig.**
The adoption of Digital Marketing has increased the sale of our business.	Between Groups	232.090	4	58.023	116.457	0.000
	Within Groups	206.767	415	0.498		
	Total	438.857	419			
I received more orders after the adoption of Digital Marketing	Between Groups	225.224	4	56.306	112.467	0.000
	Within Groups	207.767	415	0.501		
	Total	432.990	419			
My sale revenue has not affected after the adoption of Digital Marketing	Between Groups	94.939	4	23.735	15.602	0.000
	Within Groups	631.308	415	1.521		
	Total	726.248	419			
I have received more queries from buyers of my products in the market.	Between Groups	55.124	4	13.781	21.425	0.000
	Within Groups	266.933	415	0.643		
	Total	322.057	419			
My customer base has been increased after opting for Digital Marketing	Between Groups	90.139	4	22.535	34.335	0.000
	Within Groups	272.375	415	0.656		
	Total	362.514	419			

Source: Primary Data through Questionnaire

4.5.5 Content Marketing

Hypothesis: $H_1^{3.5}$: There is significant impact of Content Marketing on sale of business organization.

In content marketing, out of 5 factors responsible for sale growth, all of them are significant. The f-value and the significant value of these factors are as follows the adoption of content marketing has increased business sale (f-value: 45.329, sig=0.000, ≤0.05), received more orders (f-value: 22.170, sig=0.000, ≤0.05), increased in sale revenue (f-value: 14.108, sig=0.000, ≤0.05), have started receiving more queries from buyers (f-value: 16.933, sig=0.000, ≤0.05), and increase in customer base (f-value: 31.189, sig=0.000, ≤0.05).

Table 4.25: Significance of Content Marketing with Sale of Business

ANOVA						
Statements		**Sum of Squares**	**df**	**Mean Square**	**F**	**Sig.**
The adoption of Digital Marketing has increased the sale of our business.	Between Groups	133.440	4	33.360	45.329	0.000
	Within Groups	305.418	415	0.736		
	Total	438.857	419			
I received more orders after the adoption of Digital Marketing.	Between Groups	76.233	4	19.058	22.170	0.000
	Within Groups	356.757	415	0.860		
	Total	432.990	419			
My sale revenue has not affected after the adoption of Digital Marketing.	Between Groups	86.934	4	21.733	14.108	0.000
	Within Groups	639.314	415	1.541		
	Total	726.248	419			
I have received more queries from buyers of my products in the market.	Between Groups	45.188	4	11.297	16.933	0.000
	Within Groups	276.869	415	0.667		
	Total	322.057	419			
My customer base has been increased after opting for Digital Marketing.	Between Groups	83.789	4	20.947	31.189	0.000
	Within Groups	278.725	415	0.672		
	Total	362.514	419			

Source: Primary Data through Questionnaire

The degree of freedom of the data between groups is close to 4, and with-in groups is close to 415. The total number of participants for the survey was 420; hence overall degree of freedom is close to 419 (n-1). Therefore, it can be concluded that through Content Marketing, there is an impact on business sales growth and customer acquisition.

4.5.6 Affiliate Marketing

Hypothesis: $H_1^{3.6}$: There is significant impact of Affiliate Marketing on sale of business organization.

In affiliate marketing, out of 5 factors responsible for sale growth, four of them are significant. The f-value and the significant value of these factors are as follows:

Table 4.26: Significance of Affiliate Marketing with Sale of Business

ANOVA						
Statements		**Sum of Squares**	**df**	**Mean Square**	**F**	**Sig.**
The adoption of Digital Marketing has increased the sale of our business.	Between Groups	25.692	4	6.423	6.451	0.000
	Within Groups	413.166	415	0.996		
	Total	438.857	419			
I received more orders after the adoption of Digital Marketing.	Between Groups	18.679	4	4.670	4.678	0.001
	Within Groups	414.311	415	0.998		
	Total	432.990	419			
My sale revenue has not affected after the adoption of Digital Marketing.	Between Groups	34.655	4	8.664	5.199	0.000
	Within Groups	691.593	415	1.666		
	Total	726.248	419			
I have received more queries from buyers of my products in the market.	Between Groups	5.728	4	1.432	1.879	0.113
	Within Groups	316.329	415	0.762		
	Total	322.057	419			
My customer base has been increased after opting for Digital Marketing.	Between Groups	8.029	4	2.007	2.350	0.054
	Within Groups	354.486	415	0.854		
	Total	362.514	419			

Source: Primary Data through Questionnaire

the adoption of affiliate marketing has increased business sale (f-value: 6.451, sig=0.000, ≤0.05), received more orders (f-value: 4.678, sig=0.001, ≤0.05), increased in sale revenue (f-value: 5.199, sig=0.000, ≤0.05), and increase in customer base (f-value: 2.350, sig=0.054, ≤0.05). The degree of freedom of the data between groups is close to 4, and with-in groups is close to 415. The total number of participants for the survey was 420; hence overall degree of freedom is close to 419 (n-1). Therefore, it can be concluded that through AM, there is an impact in business sales and customer acquisition. Overall, as per the writer (Bala et al., 2018), there is an experience of a fundamental change in India towards digitalization. Nowadays, consumers are more prone towards the information search on the internet. Here author acknowledged the business growth through digital marketing such as SEO, SEM, Content Marketing, Affiliated marketing, E-mail marketing etc. In the research finding, the author (Bala et al., 2018) has demonstrated the people connect with applications like Whatsapp, Facebook, Instagram, etc. In addition, he said, through social media, these opportunities create a new source of income for various other small business owners. The correlation of the sale growth could be seen in the below-demonstrated table. Therefore, from the above discussion is it clear that hypothesis H_1^3: There is significant impact of various modes of digital marketing on sale of business organization is accepted.

4.6 Most Effective Digital Marketing Mode for Business Organisations

In the study the participants were asked to rate the most effective digital marketing mode on the Likert Five-point scale.

Table 4.27: Descriptive Statistics of Most Effective Mode of Digital Marketing

Sr. No.	Digital Marketing Modes	Mean	Standard Deviation
1.	Social Media Marketing	4.410	.9134
2.	Search Engine Marketing	3.848	.9451
3.	Email Marketing	3.629	.9088
4.	Search Engine Optimization	3.724	.9721
5.	Content Marketing	3.562	.8509
6.	Affiliate Marketing	2.419	1.3165

Source: Primary Data through Questionnaire

The analysis of the collected data is discussed in the Table 4.26. The data was analysed on the basis of Mean score value and Standard deviation. From the analysed data it is found that Social Media Marketing with Mean Score and Standard Deviation (4.410; 0.91) is one of the most effective digital marketing modes, followed by Search Engine Marketing with Mean score value and Standard Deviation (3.85; 0.95). The least effective digital marketing mode was found Affiliate Marketing with Mean score value (2.42; 1.32). So, from the results we can say that business firms have chosen Social Media Marketing, the most effective mode of digital marketing. Hence the inclination of their strategies is towards the usage of social media marketing for the promotion and advertisements of their products and services.

4.7 Most Effective Social Media Channel for Business Organisations

Here in the study, participants responses have been viewed at the type of business level, wherein there are 60% Sole Proprietorship, 24.76% Corporation, 10.47% Partnership firms, and 3.8% Semi-Government. The remaining 0.95% of participants are from other firms. At the SMC level, data has been gathered in a 5-points Likert scale, wherein the breakup is as follows 1-no extent, 2-little extent, 3- neutral, 4-very much extent and 5-great extent.

Table 4.28: Descriptive Statistics of the SMC at the type of business level

SMC	Responses	Type of Business					
		Sole Proprietorship	Partnership	Corporation	Semi-Government	Others	Total
Facebook	No Extent	12(2.85%)	0 (0%)	0 (0%)	0 (0%)	0 (0%)	12(2.85%)
	Little Extent	12(2.85%)	0 (0%)	12(2.85%)	0 (0%)	0 (0%)	24(5.71%)
	Neutral	12(2.85%)	0 (0%)	16 (3.8%)	0 (0%)	0 (0%)	28(6.66%)
	Very Much Extent	156(37.14%)	44(10.47%)	60(14.28%)	8(1.9%)	4(0.95%)	272(64.76%)
	Great Extent	60 (14.28%)	0 (0%)	16 (3.8%)	8(1.9%)	0 (0%)	84 (20%)
	Total	252 (60%)	44(10.47%)	104(24.76%)	16 (3.8%)	4(0.95%)	420 (100%)

Platform							Total
Instagram	No Extent	12 (2.85%)	0 (0%)	8 (1.9%)	0 (0%)	0 (0%)	20 (4.76%)
	Little Extent	24 (5.71%)	0 (0%)	16 (3.8%)	0 (0%)	0 (0%)	40 (9.52%)
	Neutral	52 (12.38%)	0 (0%)	24 (5.71%)	8(1.9%)	0 (0%)	84 (20%)
	Very Much Extent	76 (18.09%)	40 (9.52%)	28 (6.66%)	4 (0.95%)	4(0.95%)	152(36.19%)
	Great Extent	88 (20.95%)	4 (0.95%)	28 (6.66%)	4 (0.95%)	0 (0%)	124(29.52%)
	Total	252 (60%)	44(10.47%)	104(24.76%)	16 (3.8%)	4(0.95%)	420 (100%)
YouTube	No Extent	16 (3.8%)	0 (0%)	4 (0.95%)	0 (0%)	0 (0%)	20 (4.76%)
	Little Extent	48 (11.42%)	4 (0.95%)	20 (4.76%)	0 (0%)	0 (0%)	72 (17.14%)
	Neutral	100 (23.8%)	8 (1.9%)	36 (8.57%)	0 (0%)	0 (0%)	144(34.28%)
	Very Much Extent	16 (3.8%)	20 (4.76%)	20 (4.76%)	8(1.9%)	4(0.95%)	68 (16.19%)
	Great Extent	72 (17.14%)	12 (2.85%)	24 (5.71%)	8(1.9%)	0 (0%)	116(27.61%)
	Total	252 (60%)	44(10.47%)	104(24.76%)	16 (3.8%)	4(0.95%)	420 (100%)
Twitter	No Extent	16 (3.8%)	4 (0.95%)	4 (0.95%)	0 (0%)	0 (0%)	24 (5.71%)
	Little Extent	48 (11.42%)	0 (0%)	24 (5.71%)	0 (0%)	0 (0%)	72 (17.14%)
	Neutral	128(30.47%)	20 (4.76%)	44 (10.47%)	4 (0.95%)	0 (0%)	196 (46.66%)
	Very Much Extent	12 (2.85%)	8 (1.9%)	12 (2.85%)	4 (0.95%)	0 (0%)	36 (8.57%)
	Great Extent	48 (11.42%)	12 (2.85%)	20 (4.76%)	8(1.9%)	4(0.95%)	92 (21.9%)
	Total	252 (60%)	44(10.47%)	104(24.76%)	16 (3.8%)	4(0.95%)	420 (100%)
LinkedIn	No Extent	20 (4.76%)	0 (0%)	8 (1.9%)	0 (0%)	0 (0%)	28 (6.66%)
	Little Extent	52 (12.38%)	4 (0.95%)	12 (2.85%)	0 (0%)	0 (0%)	68 (16.19%)
	Neutral	112(26.66%)	20 (4.76%)	36 (8.57%)	12 (2.85%)	0 (0%)	180(42.85%)
	Very Much Extent	12 (2.85%)	4 (0.95%)	24 (5.71%)	4	4(0.95%)	48 (11.42%)

					(0.95%)		
	Great Extent	56 (13.33%)	16 (3.8%)	24 (5.71%)	0 (0%)	0 (0%)	96 (22.85%)
	Total	252 (60%)	44(10.47%)	104(24.76%)	16 (3.8%)	4(0.95%)	420 (100%)
WhatsApp	No Extent	12 (2.85%)	4 (0.95%)	12 (2.85%)	0 (0%)	0 (0%)	28 (6.66%)
	Little Extent	60 (14.28%)	0 (0%)	20 (4.76%)	0 (0%)	0 (0%)	80 (19.04%)
	Neutral	16 (3.8%)	12 (2.85%)	24 (5.71%)	4 (0.95%)	0 (0%)	56 (13.33%)
	Very Much Extent	48 (11.42%)	8 (1.9%)	12 (2.85%)	4 (0.95%)	0 (0%)	72 (17.14%)
	Great Extent	116(27.61%)	20 (4.76%)	36 (8.57%)	8(1.9%)	4(0.95%)	184 (43.8%)
	Total	252 (60%)	44(10.47%)	104(24.76%)	16 (3.8%)	4(0.95%)	420 (100%)
Telegram	No Extent	40 (9.52%)	4 (0.95%)	48 (11.42%)	4 (0.95%)	4(0.95%)	100 (23.8%)
	Little Extent	116(27.61%)	16 (3.8%)	20 (4.76%)	0 (0%)	0 (0%)	152(36.19%)
	Neutral	48 (11.42%)	16 (3.8%)	28 (6.66%)	8(1.9%)	0 (0%)	100 (23.8%)
	Very Much Extent	0 (0%)	0 (0%)	4 (0.95%)	4 (0.95%)	0 (0%)	8 (1.9%)
	Great Extent	48 (11.42%)	8 (1.9%)	4 (0.95%)	0 (0%)	0 (0%)	60 (14.28%)
	Total	252 (60%)	44(10.47%)	104(24.76%)	16 (3.8%)	4(0.95%)	420 (100%)

Source: Primary Data through Questionnaire

Frequency distribution methods has been used to present the data in a tabular form. As per the illustrated table 4.27 discussed above, most of the sales received by the business is through the social media channel named Facebook (84.8%), Instagram (65.7%) and WhatsApp (61.0%) followed by YouTube (43.8%), LinkedIn (34.3%), Twitter (30.5%) and Telegram (16.2%). Ranking of social media channels is found on the basis of mean values which is discussed in the following Table 4.28. In this Facebook is found most effective.

Table 4.29: Ranking of Social Media Channels as per Mean Value

Social Media Channels	Mean	Rank
Facebook	3.93	1
Instagram	3.76	2
WhatsApp	3.72	3
YouTube	3.45	4
LinkedIn	3.28	5
Twitter	3.24	6
Telegram	2.47	7

Source: Primary Data through Questionnaire

Figure 4.5: Mean Values of Effective Social Media Channel

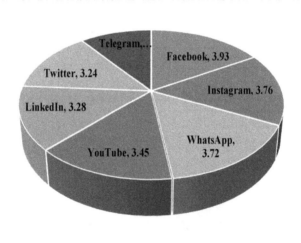

Source: Primary Data through Questionnaire

From the rating of 1 to 7 the mean and the rank of the SMC is as follows Facebook (3.93), Instagram (3.76), WhatsApp (3.72), YouTube (3.45), LinkedIn (3.28), Twitter (3.24) and Telegram (2.47). Here 1 is the highest and 7 is the lowest.

Further, to understand the significance level of the effective mode of digital marketing that influences firms below-listed hypothesis has been formed.

Hypothesis $H_1{}^4$: There are effective modes of social media marketing that influence firms to adopt digital marketing.

Here, the Pearson correlation is used to assess the significance level of the effective social media marketing channels that influence firms, where social media channels are the dependent variables and kind of business are the independent variables. Since both the parameters are parametric in nature, that is why the Pearson correlation is adopted. Here r and significance values are observed while interpreting the results at 95% confidence level. As per the results, the WhatsApp channel is not found significant with a p-value of 0.920, greater than 0.05. Further other channels such as Facebook (p-value=0.052, ≤0.05), Instagram (p-value=0.016, ≤0.05), YouTube (p-value=0.002, ≤0.05), Twitter (p-value=0.000, ≤0.05), LinkedIn (p-value=0.021, ≤0.05) and Telegram (p-value=0.002, ≤0.05) found substantial. The correlation between the type of business and the SCM channel is as follows, Facebook (25.5%), Instagram (21.7%), YouTube (14.9%), Twitter (19%), LinkedIn (11.2%) and Telegram (15.2%).

Table 4.30: Correlation between Type of Business and Social Media Channels

Correlations		Faceboo k	Instagra m	YouTub e	Twitte r	LinkedI n	WhatsAp p	Telegra m
Type of busines s	Pearson Correlatio n	0.255	0.067	.217**	.190**	.112*	-0.005	.152**
	Sig. (2-tailed)	0.052	0.016	0.002	0.000	0.021	0.920	0.002
	N	420	420	420	420	420	420	420
**. Correlation is significant at the 0.01 level (2-tailed).								
*. Correlation is significant at the 0.05 level (2-tailed).								

Source: Primary Data through Questionnaire

Hence at the overall level, it could be concluded that most effective social media marketing channel that influences firms is Facebook (25.5%), and Instagram (21.7%). Therefore, it could be said that there are effective social media marketing channels that influences firms to adopt digital marketing. **H_1^4 is accepted.**

Digital marketing is a powerful tool for all kinds of businesses. It helps in reaching prospective customer in a fraction of seconds. This could be possible because nowadays, consumers are already interrelating with various other brands through multiple social media platforms such as Facebook, Instagram, YouTube, Twitter, Linked In, WhatsApp, and Telegram. And if the brands are not interacting or speaking directly to their audience through these platforms, then they miss out on a huge opportunity. A report written by (Stream, 2018) good marketing through social media brings success to the business, drives leads and sales and also help in creating the brand.

This holds true as per the report shared by (Insight, 2018). Here the report says that among all the SMC's these are the only two channels that could give a remarkable return of investment (ROI). On Facebook, there are 1.47 billion average daily users as of June-2018.

On the other hand, Instagram is for the younger generation. This platform was launched in 2010 and usually showcased visual stories. This platform was established in 2010 but have gained popularity in 2017 only and had 8 hundred million users worldwide. In addition, the reporter said, not only for ROI, these platforms are suitable for brand engagement as well.

4.8 Customers Perception Towards Digital Marketing

Nowadays, social media is the most effective way of interaction among friends, families, consumers, buyers etc. Social media also support multiple methods for marketers to reach and engage their prospective consumers (Md.Azam Imam, Md. Zeeshan et al., 2016). In the research, attention has been made to evaluate the customers' perception towards digital marketing. Therefore, data of 563 online customers have been collected via Google form. However, while managing the data, few online users have not filled the survey form completely (3%), so missing data treatment in SPSS software has been adopted. Later on, demographic factors have been evaluated at the amount of time online users spend on the internet. A non-parametric chi-square test has been initiated to find the significance level of the considered socio-demographic factors.

Table 4.31: Significance of Demographic factors with time spent on Internet

Demographic Factors		Spend Most of the time on the internet				Pearson Chi-Square	Sig
		Disagree	Agree	Neutral	Total		
Age (in years)	< 18 years	0 (0%)	0 (0%)	4 (0.7%)	4 (0.7%)	57.915ᵃ	0.000
	18-22 years	30 (5.3%)	41 (7.2%)	8 (1.4%)	79 (14%)		
	23-27 years	75 (13.3%)	140 (24.8%)	57 (10.1%)	272 (48.3%)		
	28-32 years	22 (3.9%)	69 (12.2%)	32 (5.6%)	123 (21.8%)		
	>=33 years	26 (4.6%)	38 (6.7%)	21 (3.7%)	85 (15%)		
	Total	153 (27.1%)	288 (51.1%)	122 (21.6%)	563 (100%)		
Gender	Male	101 (17.9%)	192 (34.1%)	84 (14.9%)	377 (66.9%)	3.034ᵃ	0.552
	Female	52 (9.2%)	96 (17%)	38 (6.7%)	186 (33%)		
	Total	153 (27.1%)	288 (51.1%)	122 (21.6%)	563 (100%)		
Marital Status	Single	91 (16.1%)	189 (33.5%)	78 (13.8%)	358 (63.5%)	5.737ᵃ	0.220
	Married	62 (11%)	99 (17.5%)	44 (7.8%)	205 (36.4%)		
	Total	153 (27.1%)	288 (51.1%)	122 (21.6%)	563 (100%)		
Educational Qualifications	Graduation	76 (13.4%)	123 (21.8%)	43 (7.6%)	242 (42.9%)	23.132ᵃ	0.027
	Post-Graduation	54 (9.5%)	141 (25%)	66 (11.7%)	261 (46.3%)		
	Ph. D	2 (0.3%)	7 (1.2%)	5 (0.8%)	14 (2.4%)		
	Others	21 (3.7%)	17 (3%)	8 (1.4%)	46 (8.1%)		
	Total	153 (27.1%)	288 (51.1%)	122 (21.6%)	563 (100%)		
Occupation	Student	39 (6.9%)	65 (11.5%)	26 (4.6%)	130 (23%)	74.128ᵃ	0.000
	Professional	15 (2.6%)	101 (17.9%)	47 (8.3%)	163 (28.9%)		
	Businessman/ Entrepreneur	13 (2.3%)	29 (5.1%)	23 (4%)	65 (11.5%)		
	Government Employee	43 (7.6%)	40 (7.1%)	15 (2.6%)	98 (17.4%)		
	Consulting	43 (7.6%)	53 (9.4%)	11 (1.9%)	107 (19%)		
	Total	153 (27.1%)	288 (51.1%)	122 (21.6%)	563 (100%)		

Source: Primary Data through Questionnaire

Age: Among 563 online users, the age group of most of the users 272 (48.3%) is 23-27 years, followed by 28-32 years 123 (21.85) and >=33 years 85 (15%). There are only 14.7 of online users whose age is less than 23 years. Besides that, 288 (51.1%) users agreed that they spend time on the internet. The Chi-square(χ^2) value and the significance value of the data is 57.915[a] and 0.00. This infers that age does impact internet usage, i.e., as age grows, use of the internet increases significantly.

Gender: Regarding gender, no significant impact has been observed. The Chi-square(χ^2) and the significance value of the data is 3.034[a] and 0.552, where the practical value is greater than the tolerance limit of 0.05. There are 377 (66.9%) males and 186 (33%) females in the data.

Marital Status: Has also not shown a significant impact on the amount of time online users spend on the internet. The Chi-square(χ^2) and the significance value of the data is 5.737[a] and 0.220, where the practical value is greater than the tolerance limit of 0.05. There are 358 (63.5%) single and 205 (36.4%) married consumers.

Educational Qualification: Consumers who have participated in the survey are qualified as follows graduation 242 (42.9%), post-graduation 261 (46.3%) and Ph.D. 14 (2.4%). The chi-square (χ^2) and the significance value are 23.132[a] and 0.027, where the probability value is less than the tolerance limit of 0.05. Therefore, it can be concluded that educational qualification does play a substantial role in internet usage.

Occupation: In the collected data, consumers are from different occupations such as professionals 163 (28.9%), student 130 (23%), consulting 107 (19%), government job 98 (17.4%), and businessman or entrepreneur 65 (11.5%). The chi-square (χ^2) and the significance value are 74.128[a] and 0.000, where the probability value is less than the tolerance limit of 0.05. Therefore, it can be concluded that occupation does play a substantial role in internet usage. Hence, data concluded that users spend time on the internet as per their age, educational qualifications, and occupation. Individuals aged greater than 23 years are more prone towards internet usage. However, there is no gender and marital status impact found on time spend on the internet. In addition, statistics shared by (Statistica, 2021) reveals that the duration of the usage of daily mobile internet among consumers of the aged group in between 25-34 years has amounted to 225 minutes (3hr. & 45min.).

4.8.1 Influence of Digital Marketing on Customer Decision Making

In India, the internet usage growth has provided diverse prospects for online shoppers and marketers (Md.Azam Imam, Md. Zeeshan et al., 2016). The author further talked about the various digital marketing methods through which marketers can ensure constant online presence with minimal cost, provide immediate and measurable results, deliver high ROI, provide good communication between marketer and the customer, etc. In the research, an attempt has been made to evaluate the impact of various digital marketing methods in influencing consumer decision making. One-way ANOVA method has been adopted to assess the significance level at different digital marketing methods.

Table 4.32: Descriptive Statistics of Digital Marketing Mode

Modes	N	Mean	Std. Deviation	Skewness		Kurtosis	
				Statistic	Std. Error	Statistic	Std. Error
Social Media Marketing	563	3.52	1.513	-0.563	0.103	-1.159	0.206
Search Engine Marketing	563	3.37	1.250	-0.362	0.103	-0.887	0.206
Various App's such as educational, Video Sharing, content etc.	563	3.34	1.269	-0.346	0.103	-0.928	0.206
Ads while watching YouTube Videos or while playing games is more relevant	563	3.34	1.413	-0.377	0.103	-1.146	0.206
Advertisements in Email Inbox is more relevant/effective for advertising	563	2.79	1.237	0.105	0.103	-0.639	0.206

Source: Primary Data through Questionnaire

Here, diverse digital marketing methods are the dependent variable and consumer decision is an independent variable. In table 4.34, descriptive statistics of digital marketing methods has been calculated to know the basic features of the study data. In the data, skewness is less than 0.5; this infers that the data is symmetric, whereas kurtosis values drop in between ±1. This implies that the collected data is normally distributed (J.F Hair et al., 1961). Further mean and standard deviation has been taken wherein the average mean is 3.27, and the deviation is 1.28. Thus, not much deviation from the data has been observed in the collected data. Here, most users are neutral (3.27) in choosing various digital marketing methods to influence consumers. As per the ranking, the most preferred digital marketing mode is SMM (3.52), followed by SEM (3.37), various App (3.34), and ads via YouTube video (3.34).

Table 4.33: Influence of Digital Marketing on Consumer Decision Making

Digital Marketing Mode	Influence of Digital Marketing on Consumer Decision Making						
		Sum of Squares	Df	Mean Square	F	Sig.	Results
Social Media Marketing	Between Groups	11.360	4	2.840	3.114	0.015	Significant
	Within Groups	508.903	558	0.912			
	Total	520.263	562				
Search Engine Marketing	Between Groups	8.691	4	2.173	2.370	0.051	Significant
	Within Groups	511.572	558	0.917			
	Total	520.263	562				
Various App's such as educational, Video Sharing, content etc.	Between Groups	8.659	4	2.165	2.361	0.052	Significant
	Within Groups	511.604	558	0.917			
	Total	520.263	562				
Ads while watching YouTube Videos	Between Groups	8.755	4	2.189	2.388	0.050	Significant
	Within Groups	511.507	558	0.917			
	Total	520.263	562				
Advertisements in Email Inbox is more relevant	Between Groups	8.624	4	2.156	2.351	0.053	Significant
	Within Groups	511.639	558	0.917			
	Total	520.263	562				

Source: Primary Data through Questionnaire

Advertisement through email is considered the least effective source of influencer in consumer decision making.In the study, various digital marketing methods like social media marketing, search engine marketing, various App's such as educational, video sharing, content etc., ads while watching YouTube videos, and advertisements in an email inbox is more relevant have been looked at, wherein the ANOVA and significant values are as follows social media marketing (f-value=3.114, sig=0.015), search engine marketing (f-value=2.370, sig=0.051), various App's such as educational (f-value=2.361, sig=0.052), ads while watching YouTube videos (f-value=2.388, sig=0.050), and advertisements in an email inbox is more relevant (f-value=2.351, sig=0.053).

Figure 4.6: Preferred Digital Marketing Channels

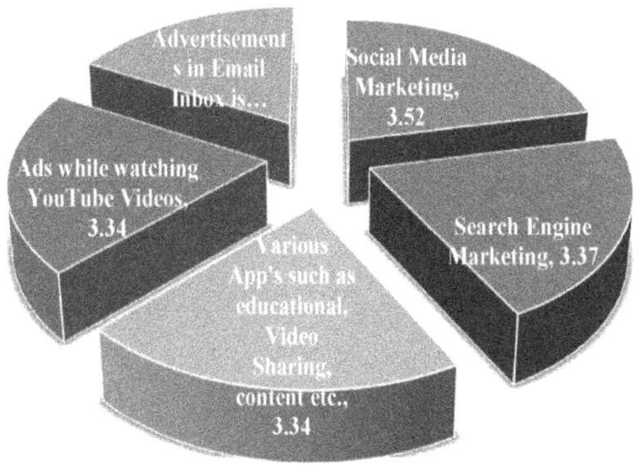

Source: Primary Data through Questionnaire

All the significant values are lesser or equal to the tolerance limit of 0.05. Hence, it can be concluded that at various digital method levels and at the overall level, digital marketing methods are influencing consumer decision making (**H₁⁵ is accepted**).

4.8.2 Customers' Perception on Influencing SMCs in Digital Marketing

According to the writer (Henderson, 2020), a social media channel (SMC) is one of the most influential and essential subsets or virtual space in the digital world. This channel is not only used for social networking but also a great source of digit advertising. Nowadays, all the big and small brands have their digital presence in almost all SMC's. This is because of the reach to respective individuals within seconds. Nowadays the consumers are thinking and making decision as per the content they find online over the internet. The reason behind this is that maximum of their time, they spend online. They are interacting, communicating online, getting their work done online, studying online. It becomes obvious to have a shift in the behaviour of consumers. This changed consumer behaviour is termed as "online consumer behaviour". It is a kind of digital revolution which is creating this changing impact on consumers as well as the business organisations.

Table 4.34: Kruskal-Wallis Test on Social Media Channel

Social Media Channel	Focus must be on Digital Marketing	N	Mean Rank	Mean	Std. Deviation	Kruskal-Wallis H	Df	Sig.	Results
Facebook	Yes	496	273.17	3.76	1.46	14.70	2	0.00	Significant
	No	6	403.33						
	Maybe	61	341.89						
	Total	563							
Instagram	Yes	496	273.62	3.74	1.47	12.38	2	0.00	Significant
	No	6	340.58						
	Maybe	61	344.39						
	Total	563							
YouTube	Yes	496	273.65	3.78	1.46	14.62	2	0.00	Significant
	No	6	432.50						
	Maybe	61	335.06						
	Total	563							
Twitter	Yes	496	288.56	2.91	1.31	7.41	2	0.02	Significant
	No	6	205.58						
	Maybe	61	236.20						
	Total	563							
LinkedIn	Yes	496	286.01	2.74	1.16	2.79	2	0.25	Not Significant
	No	6	236.92						
	Maybe	61	253.87						
	Total	563							
WhatsApp	Yes	496	288.19	3.88	1.16	6.82	2	0.03	Significant
	No	6	261.17						
	Maybe	61	233.68						
	Total	563							
Pinterest	Yes	496	279.19	2.58	1.10	1.80	2	0.41	Not Significant
	No	6	343.00						
	Maybe	61	298.88						
	Total	563							
Telegram	Yes	496	284.35	3.16	1.49	1.64	2	0.44	Not Significant
	No	6	211.83						
	Maybe	61	269.80						
	Total	563							

Source: Primary Data through Questionnaire

This way, marketers can reach out to their potential audience within few seconds at a minimal cost. Here, through this study, an attempt has been made to evaluate the customers' perception influence of SMCs on digital marketing. For the study, SMCs are the dependent variable, and digital marketing is an independent variable.

Kruskal-Wallis Test has been adopted to get the significance level wherein significant statistical difference between two or more groups of an independent variable can be evaluated. Descriptive Statistics is also used to see the mean and standard deviation of the data.

There is also a rank test used where the mean rank of the responses has been calculated. As per table 4.36 results, SMCs like Facebook, Instagram, YouTube, Twitter and WhatsApp are found significant. Kruskal-Wallis and significant values of these SMC's are as follows Facebook (KH= 14.70, sig=0.00), Instagram (KH= 12.38, sig=0.00), YouTube (KH= 14.62, sig=0.00), Twitter (KH= 7.41, sig=0.02) and WhatsApp (KH= 6.82, sig=0.03).

Figure 4.7: Preference of Social Media Channels

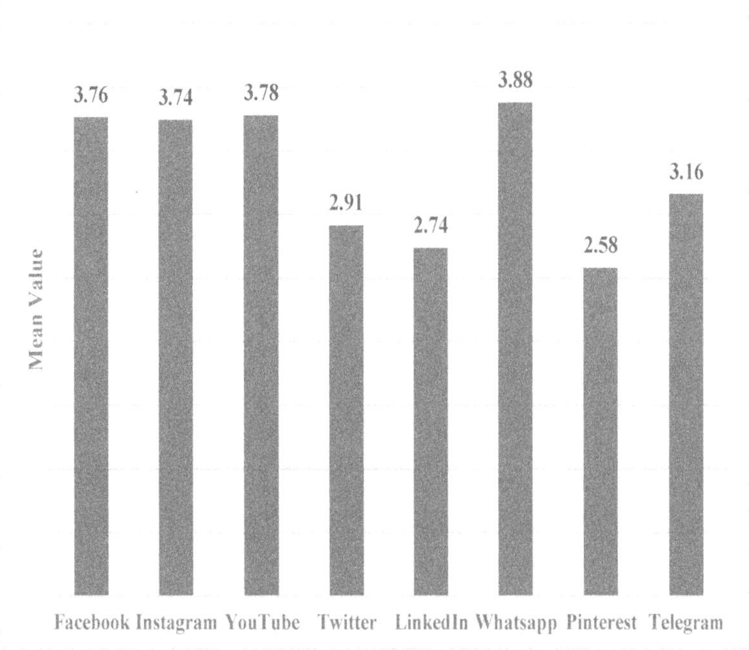

Source: Primary Data through Questionnaire

All the values are significant and less than the tolerance limit of 0.05. The mean and standard deviation of these SMC's are as follows Facebook (3.76 ± 1.46), Instagram (3.74 ± 1.47), YouTube (3.78 ± 1.46), Twitter (2.91 ± 1.30) and Whatsapp (3.88 ± 1.15). Here data infers that, as per the online users, the preference of the SMCs for digital marketing are as follows WhatsApp (3.88), YouTube (3.78), Facebook (3.76), Instagram (3.74) and Twitter (2.91). Therefore, as per the primary and secondary data, it can be said that social media channels are the most influential and essential subsets of digital marketing **(H_1^6 is accepted).**

This chapter gives a positive ending to the present study and concludes with unique findings of the study, a brief summary of the study, different implications of found results. Future aspects of the study and different suggestions to business organisations have also been discussed in this particular chapter. Basically, this chapter summarises the whole study in different aspects.

Digital marketing is innovative marketing for all kinds of businesses. Nowadays, it has come in the category of modern marketing for every business sector. Digital marketing plays a steady role in the companies' multi-channel (MC) marketing strategy. This multi-channel medium has provided advanced models and business transactions for the IFS (International Financial System). Through digital marketing, business owners have got outstanding success.

However, these business owners have to be highly careful while selecting the appropriate digital marketing strategy. Nowadays, the online platform is widely used by organizations to boost business. This is one of the most economical and successful digital marketing techniques.

5.1 Findings of The Study

The present study was mainly focused on to study the different impacts of digital marketing on Indian firms and also the customers' perception towards digital marketing. Descriptive analysis was used to present the profile of the respondents which includes frequency and the percentage values. To assess the impacts of digital marketing on Indian firms and customers' perception towards digital marketing, different statistical methods like, Factor Analysis, Reliability Test, One-Way ANOVA, Correlation, Frequency Distribution, Mean, and Standard Deviation were used.

5.1.1. a) Descriptive Analysis (Firms)

With the descriptive analysis, respondents' profiles were presented by including frequency and percentage values. The results found are discussed below:

5.1.1.1 By the results it is cleared that out of received data of 420 respondents, 252 business firms i.e., 60% were from the sole proprietorship, 104 (24.8%) were from corporations, 44

(10.5%) were from partnership, 16 (3.8%) were from semi government and 4 (1%) falls under the category of others.

5.1.1.2 Maximum of the companies, 80 (19%) were from health sector, followed by 72 (17.1%) from IT sector. There were some firms from food and hospitality, production and manufacturing.

5.1.1.3 Descriptive analysis further cleared that about 60% of the participants were using digital marketing from more than 4 years, 26.7% from 3 to 4 years and only 4.8% were making use of digital marketing from less than one year. This means maximum of the firms were experienced and compatible with the use of digital marketing.

5.1.1.4 With the help of descriptive analysis, it is also revealed that about 75.2% of the firms were agreeing that their sale revenue have increased after the adoption of digital marketing, 3.8% said no for this, and the others opted not to reveal the same. This clarifies that digital marketing is helping firms in generating more sale revenue.

5.1.1.5 If we talk about the use of well-optimized websites and social media pages, it is found that more than 90% of the firms have well optimized websites and more than 97% of the firms have social media pages.

This showed that firms are greatly investing time and efforts in the promotion and advertisements of their products and services through digital marketing channels.

b) Descriptive Analysis (Customers')

5.1.1.6 With the help of descriptive analysis, it is found that, most of the customers (48.3%) were from age group – 23-27 years, 15% were from age group more than 33 years and approx. 14% from age group less than 23 years. With this 52% were agreed for maximum time spend on Internet.

5.1.1.7 It is also found that in the list of total 563 respondents there were 377 Male participants and 186 were Female. In which approximately 64% were single and 36% were married. If we talk about education qualification and occupation approximately 43% were graduates, approx. 45% were post graduates and approx. 2 percent were in the category of Ph.D.

It is also revealed that 29% of the participants were professionals like Engineers, Doctors, or working professional in corporate sector, 23% participants were students, 17% were on Government jobs and approx. 11% were businessmen and entrepreneurs.

It is concluded from the descriptive analysis, that the users spend time on the Internet as per their age, educational qualifications, and occupation. Customers having age more than 23 years are more prone towards the usage of Internet. There is very less impact of gender and marital status found on the usage of Internet.

5.1.2 Factors Motivate to Adopt Digital Marketing

By using factor analysis and different other statistical tests like KMO, Bartletts and chi-square, the data value was found significant, which infers that the identified factors, influencing digital marketing adoption are substantial, reliable and correlated.

With this it is found that the first important motivating factor is 'Changing Customers Attitude' with factor loading of 76.3%. The second important motivating factor is organizational with factor loading 75%.

The third motivating factor is business environment with 69.3% of factor loading. The fourth and fifth motivating factors are technological and management with factor loading 65.8 and 57.6% respectively. With this our hypothesis $H_1{}^1$: (Identified factors motivate the adoption of digital marketing" was proved right. It also answered our one of the research questions that there is the role of upcoming technologies like 5G, Artificial Intelligence, Machine Learning etc. on digital marketing adoption.

5.1.3 Challenges Faced by The Firms During Adoption of Digital Marketing

Identified challenges were analysed on the basis of Mean score value and the results were found that, Data Management is the biggest challenge for firms with Mean score value 4.06, followed by Customers'/Employees' changing behaviour with mean score value 3.86 and competitive analysis with mean 3.64 and government policies with mean 3.23 found least impacted challenges. All the challenges were found significant with all the factors motivating the adoption of digital marketing by using ANOVA test.

With this the hypothesis $H_1{}^2$: "there are identified challenges in the adoption of digital marketing" proved right.

5.1.4 Impact of Digital Marketing on The Sales of Business Firms

By percentage descriptive analysis, it is found that 88.6% respondents agreed that adoption of digital marketing has increased the sales of the firms, 84.8% agreed that post digitization, they are receiving more orders online, 69.5% agreed that their sale revenue has increased, 83.8% agreed that they are receiving more product related queries, 81% agreed that their customer base has been increased.

One way ANOVA was used to analyse the significance level of impact of digital marketing modes on business growth. In all the digital marketing modes, out of the five factors responsible for sale growth, all of them are found significant. (Values can be accessed in Chapter 4)

5.1.5 Identified Social Media Marketing Channels That Influence Business Firms to Adopt Digital Marketing

For this descriptive analysis with the frequency and percentage values as well as one-way ANOVA test was used to find out the significance level.

With the help of descriptive analysis, it is found that most of the sale received by business is through Facebook (84.8%) followed by Instagram (65.7%) and least by Twitter (30.5%) with Telegram (16.2%).

So, from this it is cleared that Facebook and Instagram are the two most effective social media channels which influence the sales of business organisation more in a great way. The significance level was checked to test the framed hypothesis $H_1{}^4$, which "there are effective modes of social media marketing which influence the business organisations to adopt digital marketing". With the help of Pearson's Correlation method and it is found that except WhatsApp with p value (0.920) which is not significant. Hence all the social media channels except WhatsApp, are found significant and effective in which Facebook and Instagram found the most effective channels.

5.1.6 Customers' Perception Towards Digital Marketing

a) Influence of Digital Marketing on Customers' Decision making:

This is analysed with the help of One-Way ANOVA and Descriptive Statistics methods. It is found from the results that each digital marketing mode is significant (Values can be accessed in Chapter 4). And with this, the hypothesis $H_1{}^5$ is also proved true, i.e., the different digital marketing mode or methods influence consumer decision making.

b) Customers' Perception on Influencing SMCs to adopt Digital Marketing

Kruskal-Wallis Test was used to check the significance level between SMCs and customers' perception. It is found that according to customers' perception, Facebook, Instagram, YouTube, Twitter, WhatsApp could be the influencing Social Media Channels (SMCs) to adopt digital marketing. Since, Pinterest and LinkedIn are found insignificant, that means they are less influencing as compared to others.

From the findings of the study, it is concluded that all the major research questions or issues framed for the present study are answered or resolved successfully. Few of them are:

- All the modes of digital marketing like SEM, SMM, Email Marketing, SEO, Content marketing, Affiliate Marketing etc. are in worldwide trends and helpting business organisations to grow more.
- Changing Customers' Attitude, Management Factors, Business Environment Factors, Organzational Factors and Technological Factors are the factors motivating business organisations to adopt digital marketing.
- Use of digital marketing is easing the different marketing activities in the organisation and a very cost effective method to use for the marketing activities over the Internet.
- Business organisations are using different digital marketing strategies like Social Media Marketing, Email Marketing, Content Marketing to grow their brands.
- There are different challenges, business organisations are facing during the adoption of digital marketing like, Data Management, Customers'/Employees Changing Behaviour, Training of Staff, Selection of right strategy and technology, Analysis of competion, lack of finance etc.

- Digital Marketing is contributing in the growth of the business organisation in terms of sale, brand value and customer base etc.
- Different social media channels (SMCs) like Facebook, Instagram, Twitter, LinkedIn, WhatsApp etc. are contributing in the growth of business organisations.
- Consumers are getting influenced by the use of digital marketing platforms, as they are spending most of their time on Internet, they are expecting more services from business organisations over the Internet.
- There will be the important role of upcoming technologies like 5G, Artificial Intelligence, Machine Learning etc. on digital marketing adoption.

In the following section, suggestions, recommendations and the directions for future research on the related topic are discussed. It will be helpful in filling the gaps identified in the study.

5.2 Summary

With the continuous growth in Technology, and dominance of Internet, the maximum of the world population spending maximum of their times over the Internet. Telecom sector has played a very important role in this never-ending change. Telecom companies like R-Jio are playing an important role in this continuous transformation. There are different factors which are regularly contributing in the growth of Internet like 4G services, Technological advancements. People are preferring to do the online activities like online shopping, Internet banking, video streaming, playing games, availing food and travel services, education services etc. As the World is sitting online, the corporate sector is also shifting their business strategies towards digitalization. In 2018, India had 480 - 570 million internet users. This figure is projected to grow to 666.4 million internet users in 2023 (Source: **"Statista" - an online statistic, market research and business intelligence portal**). This has given an insight that the future of advertisement, marketing and different promotional activities is Digital Marketing.

As the secondary data from different reports, articles reveal that digital marketing is going to be the need of hour for business organisations, it becomes important to understand the point of view of the business organisations which are making use of digital marketing. For this the present study is conducted. With this the perception of customers towards digital marketing is also analysed. For the present study, a comprehensive literature review was conducted to find out the literature gap and deciding the hypothesis as well as the objectives of study on that basis. From the past studies it is found that very few researches have been conducted regarding the digital marketing in India. It is also found that the research concerns could be on different following objectives as these areas are less studied. The raised research questions and the finalised objectives for the study were:

- What are the different worldwide trends in the usage of digital marketing? Which of digital marketing tools and techniques (SEO, SEM, SMM, Email Marketing, Content Marketing, etc.) is helping the business organizations to grow more?

- What are the favorable factors towards adoption of digital marketing? How government and other forces playing a significant role in the adoption of digital marketing?

- What is the cost of campaign setup, infrastructure, and other basic requirements and facilities?

- What benefits business organizations are getting after the adoption of digital marketing? Which factors encourage business organizations most towards the adoption of digital marketing? What strategies are being used by business organizations to reap the maximum benefits of digital marketing?

- What are the challenges and benefits business organizations are facing after the adoption of the same? How digital marketing is impacting their sales, marketing share, customer relationship management, etc?

- What are the perceptions of consumers toward digital marketing? How do they perceive digital marketing? Are they influenced by digital marketing or not? Which form of digital marketing appeals most to them?

- How social media presence is important for business organizations? Businesses are getting benefits from their presence on social media channels or not. Which social media channel is more effective for business organizations like (Facebook, Twitter, Instagram, Tumblr, Whatsapp etc.)

- What will be the impact of upcoming technologies like 5G, artificial intelligence, machine learning etc. on digital marketing adoption?

- How digital marketing is influencing customers' decsion making process?

Following were the objectives decided for the present study on the basis of above research issues:

1. To study the emergence of digital marketing in the Indian scenario. (YOY secondary data analysis).
2. To identify the factors that motivates adoption of digital marketing.
3. To identify the challenges or problems faced by the firms during adoption or implimentation.
4. To measure the impact of digital marketing on the sales of business firms.
5. To identify the most effective mode of digital marketing that influences firms.
6. To analyze customers' perception towards digital marketing.

On the basis of objectives and raised research questions/concerns the following hypothesis have been framed for the present study:

H_1^1: Identified motivating factors are influencing in adoption of digital marketing for business firms.

H_1^2: There are challenges or problems faced by the firms during the adoption of digital marketing.

H_1^3: There is an impact of digital marketing modes on business growth.

H_1^4: There are effective modes of digital marketing channels that influence firms to adopt digital marketing.

H_1^5: Digital marketing does influence consumers decision making.

H_1^6: Social Media Channels are the most influential and essential subsets of Digital Marketing.

To collect the primary data, well-structured questionnaires were developed with reference to different past studies (Explained in detail in Chapter 3). Different statistical tests like Descriptive Statistics, Factor Analysis, One-Way ANOVA, Pearson's Correlation etc. were used to check the significance or relation between the independent and dependent variables. Following section will discuss the major findings of the study.

5.3 Suggestions and Recommendations

It is said that without the suggestions and recommendations, a study can not be considered complete. In this particular study, the recommendations and suggestions are for the owner of business organisations, Marketing/Digital Marketing Managers because the study will contribute for different marketing, promotional and advertisement activities.

- This research will give main idea about the different motivating factors towards the adoption of digital marketing.

- The present study can help the managers in giving insight of different challenges involved in adoption of digital marketing.

- Customers' Changing Attitude and Technological factors, Organisational, Management and Business Environment etc. are found the main factors of motivation towards the adoption of digital marketing. So, business organisation can focus more on these areas.

- The present study will give an insight about different effective modes of digital marketing. Social Media Marketing, Search Engine Marketing are found the most effective digital marketing channels for the growth of business. Business organisartions can pay more attention in the usage of these modes more efficiently.

- This study will also guide the business organisations to indetify the most effective social media channels like Facebook, Instagram, Twitter etc. which contribute more in the engagement of customers, as these channels are found most effective in the present study.

- As per customers' perception social media channels like Facebook, Instagram are more influencing. As maximum of the strategies are made keeping the customers in mind, this insight could be the most helpful for business organisations to develop or modify their strategies, because the customers role is very much important in the growth of any firm or business organisation.

- It is cleared from the customers' perception that, Price of the products/services, Timings of the dvertisements, type of adevertisement, price offers etc. are the most influencing factos in decision making. So, this insght can also be very much benficial for business organisations while developing business strategies.

- The present study identified the age group which is spending most of the time on Internet, the platforms or modes of digital marketing as well as social media marketing customers are using, type of advertisements they are linking and at what time they spent most of their hour on Internet. So, this study can suggest the business organistions to take the decsions like, whom to target (Age Group), Where to target (Platform), When to Target (Timings) and how to target (Advertisement Types). And it will become easier for organisations to adapt these strategies.

These could be some of the suggestions as well as the recommendations for business organisations which they can follow to develop their different business strategies successfully and compete with their competitors in very effective and decent way. These recommendations can be helpful for the firms or organisation of any sector as the study was not focused on a particular sector or area.

5.4 Directions For the Future Research

The present study has explained the impact of digital marketing on the growth of the business firms. But as we know that this is the time of Technological advancements, everyday we are seeing so many technological shifts and advancements and things are getting changed. In future, application and role of different upcoming technologies like Artificial Intelligence (AI), Data Science and Machine Learning (ML) in the digital marketing can be the future research aspect.

In the present study the results are from overall corporate industry but in future particular industry-wise studies could be another future research aspect. In the present study the five factors are considered for the motivational factors in the adoption of digital marketing, but in future with the help of comprehensive or systematic literature review more motivational factors in the adoption of digital marketing.

The study of those factors could be another future research aspect. These could be the few opportunities for future research. If these recommendations and directions are implemented properly, these can increase the scope of digital marketing in future. As covid-19 has impacted the business organisations at large, this could be a great opportunity to study that how business organisations have made use of digital marketing during the time of lockdown and how effective was the use of digital marketing during covid-19. The present study is an attempt to make a contribution in the field of digital marketing, which will contribute in framing different business strategies and which will be helpful in the growth of industry or business organisation.

5.5 Covid-19 and Digital Marketing

Before the outspread of the Covid-19 the business organizations and economies were growing with a great pace. But then by the end of year 2019, Corona Virus (Covid-19) has started causing its impact globally. This outspread was declared as a pandemic by World Health Organization (WHO). Covid-19 have impacted the business as well as the economic world disastrously (Ling, G.H.T., & Ho, C.M.C., 2020).

There were different corona virus outspreads in the past in different countries, but the infection and death rate of Covid-19 was tremendously higher as compared to other (Peeri et al., 2020), (Liu et al., 2020). Covid-19 have changed all the global activities drastically. In the history of mankind this is one of the drastic outspread. All the developed, developing and underdeveloped economies got affected by this pandemic as whole world was under lockdown. This outspread has created an unrest in the business world also. Many people have lost their jobs due to different reasons.

For the business organizations it was difficult to survive as the market and all the business activities were halted or minimized. There was the dire need of strategy shift for business organizations, because the strategies they were following to strive were no longer feasible. It was very difficult for the business organizations to create a real ambiance of their products or services for consumers due to lockdown or social distancing and other restrictions. Covid-19 have constrained business organizations to shift online for the advertisement and promotion of their products or services. So that they can create a strong customer base even after the lockdown situations.

CPSIA information can be obtained
at www.ICGtesting.com
Printed in the USA
LVHW080524101222
734929LV00013B/559